Revolutionaries
• Fight for Freedom •

Sanjeev Sanyal

AN ABRIDGED EDITION
FOR CHILDREN

HARPERCOLLINS
CHILDREN'S BOOKS

First published as *Revolutionaries: The Other Story of How India Won Its Freedom*
in hardback in India by HarperCollins *Publishers* 2023
This abridged edition published in India by HarperCollins *Children's Books* in 2024, 2025
An imprint of HarperCollins *Publishers* India
4th Floor, Tower A, Building No. 10, DLF Cyber City,
DLF Phase II, Gurugram, Haryana – 122002
www.harpercollins.co.in

2 4 6 8 10 9 7 5 3 1

Text copyright © Sanjeev Sanyal 2024, 2025
Illustration copyright © HarperCollins *Publishers* India 2024, 2025

P-ISBN: 978-93-5489-942-3
E-ISBN: 978-93-5489-966-9

Sanjeev Sanyal asserts the moral right
to be identified as the author of this work.

The contents of this book are for informative purposes only. The views and opinions expressed in this book are the author's own. All efforts have been made to present accurate and reliable information; however, this book is not intended to be a full account of history. The illustrations produced in this book, including the illustrated maps, flags, portraits of personalities and historical scenes, are an artistic representation meant to enhance the experience of the reader. Neither the author nor the publisher provides a warranty of any kind on the accuracy or veracity of these illustrations.

All rights reserved. No part of this publication may be reproduced,
stored in a retrieval system, or transmitted, in any form or by any means,
electronic, mechanical, photocopying, recording or otherwise,
without the prior permission of the publishers.

Inside illustrations and cover: Sanjoli C
Design and typeset: Pradnya Naik

Typeset in Spectral Font Family
Printed and bound at
Thomson Press (India) Ltd

This book is produced from independently certified FSC® paper
to ensure responsible forest management.

Contents

AUTHOR'S NOTE	4
1. THE AGE OF REVOLUTION	7
2. BHAWANI MANDIR	22
3. INDIA HOUSE	43
4. THE GHADAR	62
5. KALA PAANI	90
6. THE HINDUSTAN REPUBLICAN ASSOCIATION	117
7. CHITTAGONG	146
8. 'ONE MORE FIGHT. THE LAST AND THE BEST'	169
EPILOGUE	207

Author's Note

This book is an adaptation of my book *Revolutionaries: The Other Story of How India Won Its Freedom* (published in 2023) for younger audience (9 years and above). It discusses many events and characters that I had wondered about since childhood. Somehow, the official narrative of India's freedom struggle never quite seemed to add up. Subhas Bose was much venerated in Kolkata, where I grew up in the 1980s, but there was always some unsaid hesitancy about discussing the events related to his life. I would often stumble upon pieces of history that looked like they were important but were never spoken about. For instance, I first learnt about the Naval Revolt of 1946 in my twenties, when I chanced upon a small memorial in Colaba, Mumbai. It seemed like a major incident, but I had never read about it in history class or seen it discussed in television documentaries. Almost no one in the city seemed to know much about it. Similarly, it came as a complete surprise to me to learn that the much-revered spiritual guru Sri Aurobindo was one of the founding fathers of the revolutionary movement.

In the course of researching my earlier books, I had picked up titbits of information about the revolutionaries that I had then kept aside. Enough pieces accumulated over time for a new picture of the freedom struggle to emerge. So many books have been written about the period and about individual freedom fighters that I had assumed that the history of the freedom struggle was a settled matter. However, another narrative seemed to suggest itself at every turn. At some point, perhaps in 2014, I decided that it was worth researching the matter more systematically. For the next few years, I collected books written by those who had participated in the revolutionary movement or witnessed it first-hand. I visited sites related to them across India and the world. Eventually it became an obsession—I had to write the book.

As readers will guess, some of the characters in this book are related to me. A handful had survived into the 1980s, and I knew them personally. However, I do not claim any special knowledge merely by virtue of this. The history of the revolutionaries only began to take shape in my head after I started to systematically study them. Even the significance of first-hand anecdotes that I had heard long ago fell into place only after I started to research this book. I began to look up old letters and dusty books scattered across the family. Some of my friends began to tell me that their family members, too, had been part of the movement. They, too, shared snippets of information or put me in touch with yet other people. In this way, I was able to steadily add colour to the story.

The research led to many unexpected discoveries. For instance, by chance I found a long-forgotten box of revolutionary guns, including a Mauser C96 pistol, in the archives of Nehru Memorial Museum and Library (now Prime Ministers Museum & Library), Delhi! These are now displayed at the Biplobi Bharat Gallery in Victoria Memorial, Kolkata.

And what a story came out of the research—of unbelievable courage and ingenious plots, but also of treachery and heart-breaking failure. Moreover, it is bound up with the major global events of the twentieth century, including the World Wars, the Russian Revolution and Irish Independence.

Many people helped me put together the book. Interested readers may refer to the Author's Note in the original version for the many friends, scholars and family members who provided invaluable support with the research. Here I would like to merely highlight my editors Tina Narang, Ankita Deshpande and Shailaja Nair, who helped create this children's edition. It is no easy task to simplify a complex work while retaining the author's original language and maintaining the various interlinkages in the storyline. I would also like to thank Sanjoli C for the sketches and the cover artwork, and Pradnya Naik for the book design.

◆ 1 ◆
THE AGE OF REVOLUTION

THE DAY OF 26 August 1914 began as just another sultry monsoon day in Calcutta (now Kolkata), the second most important city of the British Empire. The city's inhabitants had known about the gathering war in Europe. This had stoked the ambitions of a network of young revolutionaries, who saw it as an opportunity to throw off the colonial yoke through armed insurrection. However, they were also aware that their supply of guns was hopelessly inadequate.

A few days earlier, a group of revolutionaries had received information from Srish Mitra, a mole who worked in RB Rodda & Company, a well-known British-owned arms retailer, that a large consignment of arms was to be delivered to the company. The consignment included fifty Mauser C96 semi-automatic pistols and 46,000 cartridges. These German-made pistols were considered the best and most reliable. Srish was in charge of clearing the consignment through customs.[1]

The group, which included Narendra Bhattacharya, Haridas Dutta, Srish Pal, Khagen Das and Anukul Mukherjee, met in a park and discussed how to steal the guns. The plan was as ingenious as it was simple. Around 11 a.m. on 26 August, Srish left his office and headed for Customs House with the money and documents needed for the receipt of the arms consignment. After being cleared through customs, the consignment was to be loaded on to six bullock carts, which would carry the goods to the company warehouse. However,

[1] Uma Mukherjee, *Two Great Indian Revolutionaries*, Dey's Publishing, 2004.

the revolutionaries had arranged for a seventh bullock cart, driven by Haridas Dutta disguised as a Hindi-speaking driver. He was dressed in a shabby dhoti and a 'genji' vest, a brass locket round his neck. He had also cropped his hair short. Srish then ordered the loading of the crates. Most of the consignment was loaded on the six official bullock carts, but the Mausers and their ammunition were loaded on the seventh.

The convoy of bullock carts made its way to the warehouse while Anukul and the others followed on foot at a safe distance. One by one, the six carts turned into the lane leading to the warehouse, but the seventh went straight. Srish reported to his superiors with the six official bullock carts. He then calmly went to the railway station and left the city by *Darjeeling Mail* that evening.

Meanwhile, the others unloaded the stolen boxes at an iron stockyard before taking them by a hackney carriage through the monsoon drizzle to the home of Bhujang Bhushan Dhar at 3 Jellapara Lane. Here the Mausers and the ammunition were divided up into smaller steel trunks for easier transportation. The original packaging and papers were destroyed and the evidence cleaned up. Some of the trunks were distributed to different revolutionary cells while the rest were hidden in warehouses owned by Marwari merchants across the city.

It took Rodda & Co. two days to realize what had happened and alert the police. The homes of suspected revolutionaries and the Marwari men's hostels were raided and searched. Eventually a number of Mausers were retrieved, including one box hidden in a warehouse owned by the well-known industrialist Ghanshyam Das Birla. He would always maintain that he knew nothing about it. Several of the conspirators were imprisoned over the next few years, but Srish disappeared without a trace.

Over the next few months, Mausers would find their way into the hands of revolutionaries across Bengal and beyond. Three of them would be used by Bagha Jatin and his companions at the famous gun battle near Balasore, Odisha. One of them would be kept for personal protection by Rashbehari Bose, the chief planner of the Ghadar uprising. He would give it to his deputy, Sachindra Nath Sanyal, just before he escaped to Japan in 1915.[2]

The Revolution of Ideas

The revolutionary movement was a result of several social and intellectual reforms. After the revolt of 1857–58, the British had militarily pacified the country and most Indians were forced to accept their political subjugation. However, the second half of the nineteenth century saw Indians respond in multiple ways, from a renewed interest in religion to the absorption of new ideas from the West. The Japanese victory over the Russians in 1905, the Irish War of Independence and the Russian Revolution of 1917 all added to the heady mix. Printing presses, including those in Indian languages, were making books and newspapers common as well as enabling the mass production of literature that challenged the colonial rule. The railways were facilitating networks within India, even as steam ships and the Suez Canal made it possible for middle-class Indians to routinely travel to Europe, North America and Japan. The revolutionaries were a product of all these influences.

[2] *Ibid.*

The year 1857 saw the establishment of three universities in Calcutta, Bombay and Madras (now Kolkata, Mumbai and Chennai, respectively). They were modelled on the University of London to provide Western-style education. The British had hoped that this would create an educated class that would not merely serve as useful clerks to administer their empire, but would, in time, imbibe enough of British tastes and ideas to be permanently loyal. While this project was partly successful in creating such a loyalist class, it also simultaneously exposed Indians to the European Enlightenment, the United States Declaration of Independence and the French Revolution. Thus, the same middle class that provided the loyalists also provided the bulk of the freedom fighters.

The wars that led to Italian unification and independence had a big impact on Indians. The Italian thinker Giuseppe Mazzini and the rebel general Giuseppe Garibaldi made a deep impression on young educated Indians growing up in the last decades of the nineteenth century. The next generation of revolutionaries was just as impressed by the Irish. So it should not be surprising that when Sachindra Nath Sanyal formed an umbrella organization for the Indian revolutionaries in 1923, he named it the Hindustan Republican Association, with a military wing named the Hindustan Republican Army—both names clearly inspired by the Irish Republican Army.

Another international phenomenon that strongly influenced the revolutionaries was Japan's victory over Russia in 1905. This was the first time in two centuries that an Asian country had defeated a major European power. Given the backdrop of European colonial empires, the rise of a non-white power was no small thing. It led to a movement called Pan-Asianism, which called for the unity of all Asiatic people.

Several leading Japanese thinkers were proponents of Pan-Asianism. Kakuzo Okakura, once the curator of the Imperial Art Museum, travelled to Bodh Gaya and Varanasi with Swami Vivekananda in 1902. His writings kindled a lot of interest in India. His book, *Ideals of the East*, began with the sentence 'Asia is one', and was read with interest by Indian opinion makers such as the Tagores of Bengal and Lala Lajpat Rai in Punjab.[3] Mitsuru Tomaya, the founder of the Black Dragon Society, was a big supporter of Pan-Asianism and provided backing for Indian revolutionaries, including political asylum for Rashbehari Bose when he escaped to Japan in 1915.

The ideas that impacted the revolutionaries did not all come from outside. Within India, there was a growing interest in religious reform and revival, as well as a renewed fascination with the country's long history of resistance to foreign invasion. Maharana Pratap, Guru Gobind Singh, Banda Bahadur and many other historical characters were extolled for leading the fight against tyrannical rulers. However, the figure of Chhatrapati Shivaji was particularly popular. His guerrilla tactics against overwhelmingly stronger enemies and his daring escape from Emperor Aurangzeb's clutches were an obvious inspiration for revolutionaries, who saw themselves in very similar circumstances. The great poet of Bengal, Rabindranath Tagore, wrote the following lines in Shivaji's honour:

---

[3] *Subhas: A Political Biography*, Sitanshu Das, Rupa Publications, 2006.

> *In what far away century, on what unmarked day*
> *We no longer know today*
> *Upon what mountain peak, in darkened forests,*
> *O King Shivaji,*
> *When did this thought light up your brow like a flash*
> *'Under one dharma, the scattered lands of Bharat*
> *Shall I unite together into One.'* [4]

The nationalist writings in both English and Indian languages in many parts of the country over the first two decades of the twentieth century reflect similar sentiments. Many of them present contemporary freedom fighters as the torchbearers of a spark lit by Shivaji. Aurobindo Ghosh wrote an imaginary conversation between Shivaji and Aurangzeb's Hindu general, Jai Singh, after they were both dead. The two argue about what they had done during their lives. The conversation ends with these powerful lines from Shivaji: *'I undermined an empire, and it has not been rebuilt. I created a nation, and it has not yet perished.'* It would have been clear to all readers that the empire to be undermined was no longer Mughal but British.

The Revolt of 1857–58 was also an important source of inspiration. While in London, Savarkar wrote a book, *The Indian War of Independence 1857*, that presented the characters and events in terms of a national revolution rather than as a mere 'mutiny', as the British preferred to present it. The book made two important points. First, it stressed the importance of Hindu–Muslim unity. Second, it argued that the key to undermining British power was to trigger a revolt among the Indian soldiers who served them. The events of 1857 were therefore seen as a dry run for the real

---

[4] First verse of Rabindranath Tagore's *Shivaji Utsav* (A Celebration of Shivaji). Translated by the author.

thing. The colonial experience was not just about political and economic subjugation but also sociocultural subjugation. With their cultural practices mocked as backward and the activities of Christian missionaries growing, both Hindus and Muslims felt uneasy. The Revolt of 1857, therefore, was partly driven by religious concerns. Colonial-era narratives particularly targeted Hindus as idolatrous heathens steeped in superstition. This led to a variety of responses, and Bengal was its epicentre. One of the responses was led by Raja Ram Mohan Roy, who attempted a formulation based on Vedantic monism. This led to the foundation of the Brahmo Samaj in Calcutta in 1829. Combined with a push for social reform, the Brahmo Samaj tried to create a version of Hinduism that was easier to defend against the criticism of contemporary Christian missionaries. Not surprisingly, this was opposed by the orthodox, who accused the Brahmos of bending too far to conform to Western sensibilities.

The debates between these two sides had important implications for Indian society. There was, however, a third group, which would prove to be even more influential in the longer run. These were the revivalist modernizers. They agreed with the Brahmos on the urgent need for reform, especially on social issues, but saw no need to be apologetic about ancient rituals and idol worship. One of the key figures of this movement was Rani Rashmoni (1793–1861), a wealthy landowner and canny businesswoman, who pushed back against the colonial government's undue intrusions into religious life and generously funded temples, bathing ghats and scholarship. One of the temples she built was the Dakshineshwar Kali temple, north of Calcutta, where she invited the remarkable, if unorthodox, saint Ramakrishna Paramahansa. His disciple, Swami Vivekananda (1863-1902), articulated a more confident Hinduism to the world, which was comfortable with both modernity and its ancient roots. Although Swami Vivekananda was not a political figure, his rekindling of civilizational confidence had a huge impact across India and the political spectrum. Virtually all branches of the revolutionary movement would come to regard him as an inspirational figure.

Other parts of India also experienced important religious developments. Punjab saw the rise of the Arya Samaj and of the Sikh reform movement. The Muslim community, similarly, experienced the modernizing Aligarh movement as well as the rise of pan-Islamic ideologies. In Maharashtra, Tilak popularized the Ganapati festival and turned it into a community event, open to all sects and castes.

All these religio-cultural changes had an impact on the revolutionaries, many of whom were deeply religious. Most of the revolutionary groups developed elaborate initiation rites infused with Hindu symbolism. When Aurobindo Ghosh initiated his brother Barin into the movement, it was done in a solemn ceremony, where Barin swore with a sword in one hand and a Bhagawad Gita in the other, that he would fight to the death for India's freedom.[5] It was common for these initiation rites to involve a vow made in front of a form of Adi-Shakti (Mother Goddess) such as Durga, Kali or Bhawani. Indeed, many nationalists, including non-revolutionaries, would come to view India itself as Goddess Bharat Mata (or Mother India). The song Vande Mataram (also spelt 'Bande Mataram') by Bankim Chandra Chattopadhyay explicitly extolls the motherland in the form of a goddess.

This rendition is based on Abanindranath Tagore's painting of Bharat Mata, 1905.

---

[5] Peter Heehs, *The Lives of Sri Aurobindo*, Columbia University Press, 2008.

Infused with Shakta imagery, the song became the anthem of the freedom movement.

The strong influence of the Hindu-Sikh imagination on the revolutionary movement does not mean that non-Hindu/Sikh members were not welcome. Far from it—the revolutionaries welcomed several nationalists from other religions. Many of the views held by the likes of Tilak, Savarkar and Bismil mark them out as Hindu nationalists, but their most trusted lieutenants were non-Hindus—Joseph Baptista, Madam Bhikaji Cama and Ashfaqullah Khan, respectively.

The last two decades of the freedom struggle saw the rise of a new set of ideas derived from communism. Until the Bolshevik Revolution in Russia (1917–23), virtually no one in India knew much about communism and Marxism. The term 'socialism' was more commonly used, but it had a general anti-imperialist connotation and did not denote a defined political or economic ideology. It was only in the 1920s that a handful of educated youth began to take an interest in Marxist ideas. For instance, Bhagat Singh was influenced by Marxism in the last couple of years of his life. Senior leaders of the movement such as Sachindra Nath Sanyal were, however, well known for being vehemently opposed to Marxism.

The growth of communism in the 1930s happened due to a surprising factor: the systematic indoctrination of nationalist revolutionaries in jail by the British authorities. There is more than enough evidence of how Marxist literature was supplied to political prisoners and how jailors would personally encourage the conversion. British intelligence was deliberately trying to create a wedge in the revolutionary movement, but it was a risky strategy. Despite the hold of British communists over the Indian movement, there was always the danger of creating a pathway for Russian influence. In the end, however, it paid back handsomely during the Second World War as the communists collaborated with the British against Gandhi's Quit India Movement of 1942 as well as their former revolutionary colleagues.

The Safety Valve

The Revolt of 1857 had a profound impact on the British as well, even if the official line downplayed it as a mere mutiny. Moreover, the death of between 5 and 9 million Indians in the famine of 1876–78 led to growing murmurings of dissatisfaction in the early 1880s. British officials such as Allan Octavian Hume of the Indian Civil Service (ICS) grew increasingly concerned about how this could lead to a new uprising. Hume evidently went through seven volumes of ground reports that suggested that there was an 'imminent danger of a terrible outbreak'.[6] Hume retired in 1882 and dedicated the next few years to creating a safety valve. He had the blessings of Lord Dufferin, the new governor general of India.

Hume reached out to several leading educated Indians of the time, and began to build a common platform. This led to the formation of the Indian National Congress in December 1885, the first conference of which was held in Bombay. It included seventy-two carefully chosen delegates from different parts of India. Hume made sure that Surendranath Bannerjea, then considered the leading voice of educated Indians, was not made the president of the Congress. Instead, barrister Womesh Chander Bonnerjee was elected as the first president. As historian R.C. Majumdar puts it, 'The selection

[6] *British Paramountcy and the Indian Renaissance, Vol. II*, edited by R.C. Majumdar, Bharatiya Vidya Bhawan, 1965 (reprinted 2018).

of W.C. Bonnerjee as the president of the first Congress gives a fair idea of the political outlook of the founders of the Congress. Mr Bonnerjee lived the life of an Englishman and not only kept himself aloof from, but almost ridiculed, all sorts of political agitation.'[7]

The speeches and statements of the early Congress leaders were embarrassingly servile. The writer Bankim Chandra Chattopadhyay mocked the Congress as a group of 'beggars' that had no connect with the wider population.[8] It is a good illustration of the law of unintended consequences that such an organization, created deliberately to subvert Indian aspirations, would later become an important part of the freedom struggle.

The INC began to grow beyond its debating society origins in the late 1890s due to the emergence of new leaders, in particular Bal Gangadhar Tilak, who were capable of putting forward Indian demands with new aggression. Using the Ganapati festival, Tilak began to mobilize people in Maharashtra. Along similar lines, he inaugurated the Shivaji festival in Raigad, Pune, in 1896. It saw an outpouring of songs, plays and lectures celebrating the Maratha empire. Tilak would soon find allies in Lala Lajpat Rai from Punjab and Bipin Chandra Pal from Bengal. The Lal–Bal–Pal trio would articulate a more clearly nationalist line in the first decade of the twentieth century.

Economic deprivation was an important driver of this new nationalism. The 1890s was a time of great economic hardship. *The Lancet*, a well-known medical journal, estimates that around 19 million Indians died in famines during the decade.[9] The imperial authorities and the general public in Britain were aware of these events, as they were routinely

[7] *Ibid.*
[8] *Ibid.*
[9] Sugata Bose, *His Majesty's Opponent: Subhas Chandra Bose and India's Struggle against Empire*, Penguin India, 2011.

reported in London newspapers. However, the debate was usually about the need for ramping up 'charity', not the reversal of economic policies or providing Indians more say in the government.

Less appreciated is the impact of epidemics in nineteenth-century India. These were partly caused by a famine-weakened population exposed to the large-scale movement made possible by steam-driven railways and ships. However, it was also caused by the breakdown of the traditional medical system. For instance, Indians had long practised a form of mass inoculation for smallpox, done by a network of travelling 'tikadars (vaccinators)'. After Edward Jenner published his seminal paper on smallpox vaccination in 1798, the British quickly spread the technology. The first modern vaccination in Bombay was carried out just four years later. To spread the imported vaccine, the East India Company banned the traditional system in 1804, even though these vaccines would continue to be dependent on imports from England for several decades. Although the new system steadily improved and eventually became more effective than the traditional one, the breakdown of the old system meant that a large part of the population was now left out. With epidemics becoming more common, it is not surprising that Indians were suspicious of what the colonial administration was doing.

The First Shot

The famines, epidemics and the political mobilization by Tilak provide the broader political context for an incident in June 1897 that is often said to be the first act in a new cycle of armed resistance. A plague was raging through Poona (now Pune) and the colonial authorities had just given themselves new powers under the Epidemic Diseases Act, 1897. Poona's chief plague commissioner, Walter Rand, by all accounts, exercised his powers in a most draconian manner. Soldiers raided homes and burnt down property, molested women and desecrated shrines. Plague victims were forced to vacate homes and move to quarantine centres with no food or facilities. Epidemics were not new, and Punekars would have normally accepted stern measures, but Rand's tyrannical behaviour managed to alienate the average citizen. Tilak bitterly criticized the government in his column in *Kesari*.

Two brothers, Damodar Hari Chapekar and Balakrishna Hari Chapekar, decided to assassinate Rand. It was 22 June 1897, the Diamond Jubilee of Queen Victoria. Rand had gone to attend an official event at the Government House. Armed with pistols, Damodar and Balakrishna hid at a spot on Ganeshkhind Road and waited for Rand to return home. It was completely dark when they saw an official carriage coming down the road. Balakrishna leapt at the horse-drawn carriage and shot the occupant point-blank. It was only then that he realized it was not Rand but his lieutenant Charles Ayerst. Meanwhile, another carriage came out of the darkness—the one in which Rand was travelling. Damodar attacked the second carriage and shot Rand. He was rushed to the hospital but died a few days later.

The incident shook British officials across India, and a large bounty of Rs 20,000 was offered for information. The Dravid brothers, former associates of the Chapekars, came forward and provided leads. Damodar and Balakrishna were arrested and hanged. Tilak was arrested too. Although no direct link could be established, he was sent to prison for incitement of violence. It made him a national figure.

The Chapekar brothers perhaps marked the beginning of the revolutionary movement in India. They were certainly influenced by the political forces unleashed by Tilak, but they were neither members of a significant network, nor did they have any longer-term political objectives. They merely wanted to punish Rand. However, they did inspire a new generation of Indians to take up arms. When a teenage Vinayak Savarkar learnt of the execution of Damodar Chapekar, he went to his family temple and swore in front of Goddess Bhawani that he would commit his life to freeing India of foreign rule through armed struggle. Together with Aurobindo Ghosh, Savarkar would build the intellectual basis of the revolutionary movement.

♦ 2 ♦
BHAWANI MANDIR

ONE OF THE founders of India's freedom movement, Aurobindo Ghosh was born in Calcutta on 15 August 1872 to a civil surgeon, Dr Krishna Dhun Ghosh, and his wife, Swarnalotta. The Ghosh family were members of the Brahmo Samaj. At the time of Aurobindo's birth, the community was going through a bitter split. On one side were mainstream Brahmos, who continued to think of themselves as Hindu reformers—Swarnalotta's family belonged to this camp. On the other side was a group led by Keshub Chander Sen, who wanted to become more Western to be able to ingratiate themselves with the British rulers. Krishna Dhun belonged to this group. The tension between the two strands would have a profound impact on Aurobindo.

The doctor gave Aurobindo an English-style middle name, Akroyd, and forbade the use of Bengali at home so that his children would grow up speaking only English. The only Indian language Aurobindo learnt as a child was Hindi from the household servants.[1] In 1877, when he was barely five years old, Aurobindo was packed off with his siblings to a missionary school in Darjeeling called Loretto House, run by Irish nuns. In 1879, Krishna Dhun took his family to England, where he left seven-year-old Aurobindo and two of his siblings in Manchester with Reverend William Drewett and his wife, so that they could be brought up as proper Englishmen. The Drewetts were strictly instructed that the boys 'should not be allowed to make acquaintance with any Indian or undergo any Indian influence'.[2] Thus, Aurobindo grew up with almost no contact with his native language, culture or religion.

[1] Peter Heehs, *The Lives of Sri Aurobindo*, Columbia University Press, 2008.
[2] *Ibid*.

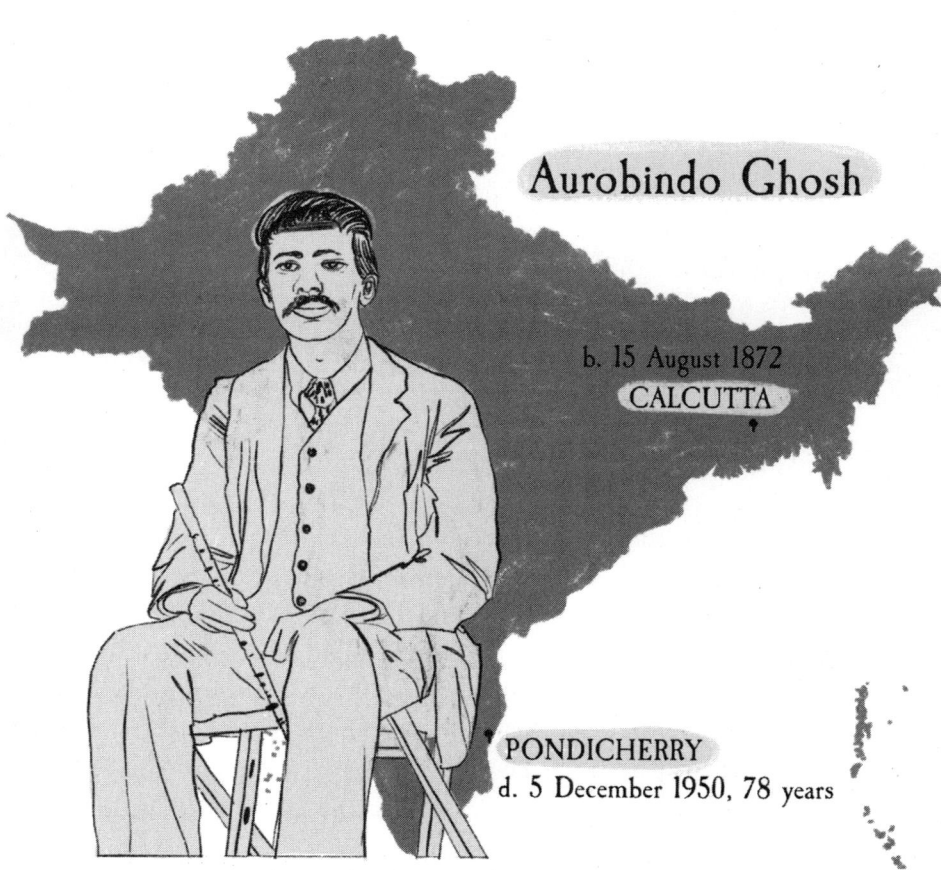

Aurobindo Ghosh

b. 15 August 1872
CALCUTTA

PONDICHERRY
d. 5 December 1950, 78 years

It was Krishna Dhun's ambition that his sons join the ICS and return to India as part of the ruling class. Aurobindo, unlike his brothers, was intellectually gifted. In December 1889, he went to Cambridge to sit for the King's College scholarship examinations. All day he did translations to and from Latin and Greek, answered questions on classical history and grammar and wrote essays in English.

Aurobindo started his education at King's College in October 1890. His scholarship entitled him to free tuition, certain privileges and a modest £80 a year. He was there to earn a degree in the classics, but his real objective was to prepare for the ICS examinations. This is why he began to study Hindu and Muslim customs, the civil and criminal procedures of British India, Sanskrit and Bengali. It was the first time that he had learnt anything related to his country of origin. Although he initially struggled, the sudden exposure to his own culture made a deep impression on the young man.

The two years in Cambridge were happy ones for Aurobindo. He had full intellectual freedom and read widely, beyond what was needed for his degree or the ICS entrance exams. He left King's with a first in the Tripos but without a degree. He had passed the preliminary ICS examinations and needed to move to London in May 1892 for the final examinations. It was during this summer that Aurobindo was exposed to the emerging political trends in India. London had a significant Indian community of all classes, including students, and they talked to the young ICS aspirant about what was happening back home. There is evidence that he and his brothers attended a meeting of a secret society dedicated to liberating India, called the Lotus and Dagger. Nothing else is known about this society.

In October, ICS examiners wrote to inform him about the final formality of a riding test. The test was compulsory and the date was set for 26 October. Aurobindo shocked everyone by refusing to take it. He was removed from the list. Something had snapped inside the talented young man who had been driven all his life by his father to join the ICS. Krishna Dhun did not survive this disappointment and died suddenly in December—some say due to heartbreak.

At the time, Sayajirao Gaekwad III, the maharaja of Baroda, was visiting London. After a brief meeting at the Savoy, Gaekwad hired Aurobindo for the civil service of his own princely state. In January 1893, after fourteen years, Aurobindo sailed back to India.

∞ The Prince Who Would Not Bow ∞

Under Sayaji's rule, Baroda had witnessed major social reforms, huge investments in industry and the founding of the Bank of Baroda. He also spent liberally on building schools, colleges and libraries. He would go on to provide generous financial support to many talented Indians of that era, including Dr B.R. Ambedkar and, of course, Aurobindo Ghosh. At a time when most Indian princes were wary of displeasing the British, Sayaji sailed close to the wind. One incident in 1911 illustrates this trait.

The Delhi Durbar of 1911 was a grand affair, the first time a ruling British monarch was visiting India. All the Indian princes were expected to pay homage to King-Emperor George V. They had to walk up to the throne in full regalia and pay obeisance by bowing three times. Then they were expected to back away without turning. As the third most senior prince after Hyderabad and Mysore, Sayaji got his turn early—but he broke all the rules. First, he refused to wear the full regalia. Then he walked up to the dais and made a single perfunctory bow, before turning around and walking off, showing his back to the emperor. This was a brave act of defiance. No one

who had witnessed the event was left in any doubt about what he had done. A witness recorded that Sayaji was laughing mockingly as he walked away from the throne.[3] Motilal Nehru, one of the witnesses, wrote disapprovingly to his son Jawaharlal, 'I am sorry to say that the Gaekwad has fallen from the high pedestal he once occupied in public estimation.'[4]

---

[3] Alastair Lawson, 'Indian maharajah's daring act of anti-colonial dissent', BBC News, 10 December 2011, https://www.bbc.com/news/world-asia-16051168
[4] Sunil Raman and Rohit Agarwal, *Delhi Durbar 1911: The Complete Story*, Lotus, 2011.

Aurobindo's Discovery of India

As a civil servant, Aurobindo spent the next several years dealing with land records, revenue stamps and so on. He spent his free time reading everything from ancient Hindu epics to contemporary politics. He was acquainting himself with India. He also made his way east to meet his family. When he arrived in Deoghar, where his maternal family lived, his mother could not recognize him, and he had to prove his identity by showing her an old scar on his finger. He was warmly embraced by uncles, aunts, cousins and nephews. He developed an especially close relationship with his sister Sarojini and younger brother Barin.

Meanwhile, he was persuaded by the journalist K.G. Deshpande, his best friend from Cambridge, to write for the English section of a weekly journal called *Indu Prakash*, published from Bombay. This is the first time Aurobindo began to express his views on national issues. Writing a series called 'New Lamps for Old', he derided the tiny elite that ran the Congress for celebrating minor concessions made to them by the British. 'Our actual enemy is not some force exterior to ourselves, but our crying weakness, our cowardice, our selfishness, our hypocrisy, our moribund sentimentalism.' [5]

The young Baroda civil servant would not have been able to write like this unless he had the tacit backing of Sayaji Gaekwad. In fact, the maharaja seems to have noticed his flair for language and begun to use him to draft his speeches and letters. Aurobindo, however, did not find his work as a civil servant stimulating, and began to spend a few hours every week teaching French at Baroda College (now known as Maharaja Sayajirao University). Sometime later, when the

[5] *Ibid.*

English professor went on furlough, he became the acting professor of English.

In 1901, Aurobindo decided to get married. He insisted on a full Hindu wedding, complete with all ancient rituals. Although both sides of his family were Brahmos, Aurobindo wanted to make a point. He felt that despite its contributions to social reform, Brahmoism was a cultural and intellectual dead end—'a rehash of that pale and consumptive shadow, English Theism'.[6] When the newly married couple returned to Baroda, the maharaja gave Aurobindo a lot of new responsibilities, including that of writing his biography. The two became quite close and began to develop a more radical anticolonial worldview.

Anushilan Samiti

Since ancient times, India has had a tradition of local gymnasiums, known as *akhadas,* which functioned as a system of imparting both military and spiritual training. They were usually places where young men were taught wrestling, the use of the sword, archery and so on. Most of them were affiliated to a Hindu religious order or a temple. In the middle ages, the akhadas played an important role in mobilizing local resistance against the Turkic conquest.

When the East India Company was attempting to conquer India, it occasionally faced resistance from the akhadas. Once in power, the British systematically defanged them. This was not difficult, as changes in military technology and training had made them obsolete. The larger networks were encouraged to become purely religious institutions. Many of the akhadas that today gather for the Kumbh Mela

[6] Peter Heehs, *The Lives of Sri Aurobindo*, Columbia University Press, 2008.

are remnants of these quasi-military orders. Meanwhile, the local akhadas gradually became more like sports clubs, teaching wrestling and other traditional forms of martial arts. In the late nineteenth century, the military purpose of the akhada network was still fresh in everyone's memory. As a more aggressive nationalism began to take root, some Indians began to wonder if akhadas could be used to build a network of secret societies that would work towards armed insurrection against the British.

Aurobindo was exploring this idea around the time that the Chapekar brothers killed Walter Rand. It was also at this time that a certain Jatindranath Banerji visited him in Baroda. Aurobindo arranged for Jatindranath to join the Baroda army to gain some military training. In 1901, Jatindranath returned to Calcutta to set up an akhada. He also began to link up with other akhadas that harboured nationalist ideas. One of these was a wrestling club called Anushilan Samiti, set up by Satish Chandra Bose, a follower of Swami Vivekananda and his Irish disciple Sister Nivedita.

In 1902, Aurobindo made a trip to Bengal to meet the people involved in the growing network. Within a year, new nodes had started popping up across Bengal and the name 'Anushilan Samiti' came to denote a wider network. Incredibly, the original club still exists in north Kolkata, but seems to specialize in badminton these days. There are no obvious signs of its link to India's freedom movement, except a large map of undivided India painted in blue and white behind the badminton court.

Meanwhile, in Baroda, Sayaji kept pushing the boundaries. In a speech written by Aurobindo and delivered in December 1902 at an industrial exhibition, Sayaji contrasted the poverty in India with the energy and prosperity in Europe. He then blamed it on the lack of a risk-taking culture and scientific knowledge, but most of all on 'the result of acquisition of political power by the East India Company and the absorption of India in the growing British Empire'. He then stated that India needed a 'great national movement', although carefully couching it as a social rather than a political programme.

To understand why this was so bold, one needs to see the contrast between Sayaji's speech and the statements made a week later at the annual conference of the INC. One of the first speakers proclaimed that 'it is for our benefit that British power should continue to be supreme in our land'. Surendranath Bannerjea, who had now managed to become the president, stated, 'We plead for the permanence of British rule in India.'[7] Aurobindo attended the conference, and it was here that he met Bal Gangadhar Tilak. Given their shared antipathy for the servile behaviour of the mainstream Congressmen, there was an instant bond between the two.

It was also around this time that Barin Ghosh came to spend some time with his brother in Baroda. He was soon deeply inspired by the idea of creating a network of revolutionary akhadas. In early 1903, in a solemn secret ceremony, Aurobindo initiated him into the Anushilan Samiti. Holding a sword in one hand and a Bhagawad Gita in the other, Barin swore that he would dedicate his life to freeing India from foreign occupation. Barin then returned to Bengal and, over the next two years, travelled across the province, setting up branches of the Anushilan Samiti.

On his part, Aurobindo wrote a tract, 'Bhawani Mandir', where he explicitly laid out the idea of building a Bhawani temple-school at a secluded location in the hills, where a

[7] *Ibid.*

generation of warrior monks could be trained. The idea was that they would spread across India and trigger the coming insurrection. The tract expressed the need to build a temple dedicated to Bhawani Bharati and provided details of how an order of warrior monks was to be established. Aurobindo began to scout for a suitable location. He decided on the town of Karnali, near Chandod, on the banks of the Narmada. The town already had an ancient temple to Goddess Kali and was within striking distance of Baroda. His journalist friend Deshpande, then assistant collector of the district, even started a pilot project in the area called Ganganath Bharatiya Vidyalaya, a school where the students could be taught both Sanskrit and modern nationalist ideas. Sayaji Gaekwad was almost certainly aware of what was happening, but was careful not to establish any direct links.

Meanwhile, Aurobindo became the vice principal of Baroda College and, with the principal away on leave, was the person in charge. He also moved into a beautiful bungalow, which has been preserved beautifully by the Sri Aurobindo Ashram and is now run as a meditation centre.

In 1905, there was a new twist to the story of India's freedom movement. Lord Curzon announced in October that Bengal would be partitioned for administrative efficiency. However, it was clear from the way the division was done that it was at least partly driven by political considerations. East Bengal would now have a Muslim majority while the Bengali Hindus of the western half would be diluted by the inclusion of a large number

of Biharis and Odiyas. Thus, the politically assertive Bengali Hindus would be weakened by religious and linguistic counterweights.

Such an obvious attempt at divide-and-rule was met with strong protests. In Calcutta, all business was suspended, shops were shuttered and vehicular traffic stopped. Large crowds marched down the streets, singing *Vande Mataram*. On 16 October, mass rakhi-bandhan ceremonies were conducted and many people across Bengal tied rakhis on each other's wrists as a symbol of their unbreakable bond. At a public meeting that attracted fifty thousand people, poet Rabindranath Tagore and veteran politician Ananda Mohan Bose made a passionate proclamation:

> 'Whereas the Government has thought it fit to effectuate the partition of Bengal in spite of the universal protest of the Bengali nation, we hereby pledge and proclaim that we, as a people, shall do everything in our power to counteract the evil effects of the dismemberment of our province and to maintain the integrity of our race. So God help us.'[8]

An important innovation of the 1905 protests was the idea of Swadeshi—the boycott of British-made goods in favour of locally made ones. This idea spread quickly across Bengal and the rest of the country. British-made clothes and other goods were thrown into bonfires. The cobblers of Mymensingh vowed that they would not mend British-made shoes, the washermen of Kalighat promised that they would no longer wash foreign-made clothes and Brahmin priests refused to officiate at marriage ceremonies where foreign-made clothes were worn.

The key Bengali leader who emerged from this was Bipin Chandra Pal, who soon received strong backing from Tilak in Maharashtra and Lala Lajpat Rai in Punjab. This was the genesis of the Lal–Bal–Pal trio.

It should be noted that the original idea of Swadeshi was not about a return to pre-modern manufacturing. We have this mental association today because of the popularization of the charkha, the hand-turned spinning wheel, by Mahatma Gandhi at a later date. The original idea was a more general expression of economic nationalism that included rapid modernization. The mood of the times led to a flurry of Indian entrepreneurs entering new fields hitherto dominated by foreign businesses. Bengal, for example, witnessed the setting

[8] *Struggle for Freedom*, edited by R.C. Majumdar, Bharatiya Vidya Bhavan, 1969.

up of Calcutta Chemicals (producers of the Margo soap), Mohini Mills (cotton textiles) and Indian Tea & Provisions (survives today as Luxmi Tea).

Barin Ghosh, meanwhile, had been setting up branches of the Anushilan Samiti across Bengal. The protests led to a sudden increase in young recruits. Branches were independently sprouting even outside Bengal. Aurobindo realized that he had to shift to Bengal to be in the thick of things. So, in early 1906, he resigned from Baroda College and moved to Calcutta. He and Barin set up a newspaper called *Jugantar* (The New Era) to spread nationalist ideas. It soon had a dedicated following, and Bhupendra Nath Dutta, Swami Vivekananda's younger brother, became one of its editors. Leaving Barin and his associates to run the paper, Aurobindo busied himself with the setting up of the National College in Calcutta as an alternative to the British- and missionary-controlled institutions. It opened in July 1906 with Aurobindo as its first principal. The college would evolve into today's Jadavpur University.

Around the same time, Bipin Pal also started a newspaper provocatively named *Bande Mataram*. He invited Aurobindo to write regularly for it. The paper quickly became popular and Aurobindo's hard-hitting editorials generated a lot of debate. Gandhi, in faraway South Africa, and Jawaharlal Nehru, in England, would comment on them. British intelligence in India read them carefully and tracts were quoted in *The Times* in London. An obscure civil servant from Baroda had become one of the most influential thinkers in the capital of British India. He had triggered a rapidly expanding revolutionary network, created a nationalist institution and was now driving the political conversation. There was also no doubt from his writings that he supported the Lal–Bal–Pal trio, which had started to challenge the old, cosy club that ran the INC.

The friction between the two factions is usually referred to as the rivalry between 'extremists' and 'moderates'. However, since this book is written from the perspective of the revolutionaries, they will be referred to as the Nationalists and the Loyalists, respectively. This is how Aurobindo referred to them.[9]

The INC conference of 1907 was originally to be held in Nagpur but Loyalist leaders Pherozeshah Mehta and Gopal Krishna Gokhale decided to shift it to Surat to deny Tilak the advantage of home turf. The cultural divide between the two camps would have been obvious to Aurobindo and Barin when they arrived in Surat on 24 December. The Loyalists were housed in luxury tents near the podium while the Nationalists were crammed into *dharamshalas* in the city's bazaar.

The Nationalists wanted their candidate, Lala Lajpat Rai, to be elected president and for the conference to pass a resolution endorsing the continuation of the Swadeshi agitations. A compromise was reached between the two sides that Rashbehari Ghosh (not to be confused with Rashbehari Bose) of the Loyalist faction would be made president, but that many of the demands of the Nationalists would be included in the resolution. Nonetheless, Tilak had still not received a draft of the resolution when the session started the next afternoon. When he did receive it, it was obvious that none of his demands had been included. A murmur went through the Nationalist camp and led to sloganeering. Surendranath Bannerjea's speech had to be stopped and the session suspended.

[9] Note that these terms were used by Aurobindo Ghosh, although he saw it as a three-way division: Nationalists (Lal-Bal-Pal and himself), Moderates (Dadabhai Naoroji and Surendranath Bannerjea) and Loyalists (G.K. Gokhale and Pherozeshah Mehta).

It could only be resumed the next day. As Surendranath resumed his speech, Tilak sent a note to the organizers that he would second the nomination of the president but would also like to move an amendment to the proposed resolution. This was accepted. However, when Surendranath ended his speech, Tribhuvan Das Malvi proposed Rashbehari Ghosh's name, and Motilal Nehru hurriedly seconded it before Tilak could even walk up to the podium. Rashbehari Ghosh then started his presidential address. Tilak protested but was shouted down. A gang of hired goons then attacked him and dragged him off. A group of young Nationalists from Maharashtra rushed to protect him. Aurobindo and his entourage walked out even as Loyalist supporters spat at them. The split was complete. That evening the two camps held separate meetings. Aurobindo presided over the Nationalist session, with Tilak as the principal speaker.

The Garden House

The Swadeshi movement had brought in new recruits and created many branches, but Barin realized that the Anushilan Samiti had neither the know-how nor the organizational capability to do anything that would meaningfully challenge British hegemony. So, Barin decided to make the risky move of creating a physical headquarters.

For this, Barin chose a *baganbari,* or a garden house, in Maniktola, just north of Calcutta. The property belonged to a supporter and consisted of two acres of land with a dilapidated house, a couple of ponds and a small family temple. It was not as romantic as the warrior monastery originally envisaged in 'Bhawani Mandir', but it was at a practical distance from the city. The Maniktola area is today within Kolkata city. The exact location of the garden house, however, is difficult to discern as the original buildings have not survived.

At the garden house, Barin gathered a group of around twenty young recruits. Despite their enthusiasm, and the acquisition of a few small arms, they knew they did not have the know-how to carry out any serious revolutionary act. Thus, Hemchandra Das was sent to Paris in late 1906 to acquire bomb-making skills. At that time, Paris was home to anarchists and revolutionaries from across Europe. Hemchandra enrolled himself to study chemistry but spent his free time meeting activists of all kinds. He also made friends with Pandurang Bapat, who had been sent from London by Savarkar for the same purpose. The duo eventually got hold of an excellent bomb-making manual from a Russian anarchist. Hemchandra then sailed back to Calcutta with a suitcase full of information on how to run an armed rebellion, including a seventy-page translation of the Russian manual.

The revolutionaries back in Calcutta had also been hard at work. Barin had found an explosives expert in Ullaskar Dutt. A few weeks before the Congress session, the revolutionaries had managed to blow up the train carrying the lieutenant governor Sir Andrew Frazer. Although the lieutenant governor was not hurt, it had proved Ullaskar's capabilities. The acquisition of Hemchandra's manual added to their skills. The problem was that Barin was becoming reckless.

The colonial administration knew that Aurobindo's writings were evoking an upsurge of nationalist feelings across India, but the editorials in *Bande Mataram* were too carefully worded to be taken to court. So they decided to go after *Jugantar*. Its staff was questioned and some were imprisoned. This was done by a district judge named Douglas Kingsford, who had a reputation for passing harsh judgments against Swadeshi protesters. The revolutionaries decided to teach him a lesson. The authorities got wind of this and transferred him to Muzaffarpur in Bihar. Barin decided to hunt him down in Bihar.

The job was given to Prafulla Chaki and an eighteen-year-old Khudiram Bose. Armed with revolvers and a small bomb, they made their way to Muzaffarpur and spent a few days observing Kingsford. On 29 April 1908, Kingsford went to the local British club with his wife and spent an evening playing bridge with the wife and daughter of Pringle Kennedy, a barrister. Khudiram and Prafulla were waiting behind some trees on the road leading to the judge's house. Around 8.30 p.m., the foursome finished their last rubber, and the Kennedy women got into a horse-drawn carriage to head home. The Kingsfords, in an almost identical carriage, were not far behind. As the first carriage passed the trees, Khudiram jumped out of the darkness and threw the bomb in through the carriage window. Both women were fatally wounded. The two attackers then escaped in the confusion, before splitting to make their way back separately.[10] While Prafulla died soon after, Khudiram was arrested and hanged.

News of the events in Muzaffarpur reached Calcutta a day later, and the authorities had a hunch that the attacks on Frazer and Kingsford had been carried out by the same group. They zeroed in on Barin's network. Early morning on 2 May 1908, the police launched simultaneous raids at several locations across the city. Barin and several of his associates were arrested from the garden house and a lot of incriminating evidence was found, including a copy of the

[10] *Khudiram Bose vs Emperor*, Bench: Bell Ryves, Calcutta High Court, 13 July 1908.

bomb manual. They also raided Aurobindo's home in Grey Street. He was arrested, his possessions were searched and boxes full of papers were carted off to the police headquarters. All the prisoners were housed in Alipore Jail. These arrests and subsequent investigations led to Emperor versus Aurobindo & Others, popularly known as the Alipore Bomb Trials. The case attracted a lot of attention in India as well as in Britain.

Even as the trial progressed into August, the revolutionaries managed to smuggle in two revolvers. Barin arranged for these to be delivered to Kanailal Dutt and Satyen Bose. Around this time, one of the prisoners, Narendranath Goswami, agreed to reveal everything he knew about the Anushilan Samiti network. Kanailal and

Satyen decided to kill Narendranath before the network was further compromised.

They confronted him in the jail yard and shot him. They were then captured and hanged. The revolvers used to kill Narendranath are on display at the Kolkata Police Museum.

The Alipore trails resumed. The police saw Aurobindo as the kingpin behind the attacks, but could not prove a direct link between him and any act of violence. His writings in *Bande Mataram,* while bold, were carefully worded and could not be connected to any specific revolutionary deed. The judgment was delivered in May 1909. Barin Ghosh and Ullaskar Dutt were sentenced to death by hanging (later reduced to life imprisonment at the dreaded Cellular Jail in Port Blair). Many of the others were given life sentences. Incredibly, Aurobindo was acquitted.

The Saint of Pondicherry

Aurobindo emerged from prison a national hero. Sister Nivedita proclaimed him India's Mazzini. With Tilak imprisoned in Mandalay, he was the most important leader of the Nationalists. As *Bande Mataram* and *Jugantar* had been shut down by the authorities, he started a new paper called *Karmayogin* in June 1909. It was an instant hit across India and soon had Tamil, Hindi and Bengali editions. Many influential foreign visitors, such as Ramsay MacDonald, a British member of parliament and future prime minister, came to meet him. This also meant that Aurobindo was a much-sought-after speaker. Over the next few months, he delivered speeches across Bengal—Khulna, Howrah, Jhalakati, Bhawanipur and so on.[11] Large crowds attended his talks.

[11] Sri Aurobindo, Speeches: On Indian Politics and National Education, Sri Aurobindo Ashram Pondicherry, 1922 (reprinted in 2018).

It was in February 1910 that Aurobindo received information that the British authorities were about to issue a new warrant against him. He and a couple of associates made their way to River Hugli and hired a small wooden boat to take them to the French enclave of Chandernagore (now Chandannagar). Here Aurobindo was hidden by the local Anushilan Samiti unit, the same group that had smuggled the revolvers into Alipore Jail. Although the British did not have legal jurisdiction there, they had agents and informers everywhere. Nonetheless, he was able to keep in touch with Sister Nivedita, who temporarily took over the editing of *Karmayogin*.

After six weeks, Aurobindo decided to move to the larger French enclave of Pondicherry (now the Union Territory of Puducherry). He only expected to stay there for a few months before heading back into British India. However, as the months passed, he steadily drifted towards the exploration of spiritual, religious and civilizational themes. With one exception, he would never again participate actively in India's political life.

Aurobindo's change of direction may seem inexplicable, but his writings explain his reasons. He seems to have concluded that he had already accomplished his role as India's Mazzini by triggering the flame of nationalism. It was now a matter of time before the British were forced to leave. He felt that there was a more important civilizational battle that India would have to fight, that would prove much harder than just gaining political freedom. After centuries under foreign rule, Indians had come to see their own culture from the perspective of those who had conquered them. Many members of the Indian elite believed that sacred texts such

as the Vedas and the Upanishads were just superstition—like Aurobindo's father, they had come to believe modernization meant Westernization. Aurobindo felt that it was his duty to rediscover the true core of Indian civilization and present it to Indians and the wider world. With this in mind, he dived deep into the Rig Veda, the most ancient and revered of Hindu texts. Aurobindo Ghosh was well on his way to becoming Sri Aurobindo.

◆ 3 ◆
INDIA HOUSE

VINAYAK WAS BORN on 28 May 1883 to Damodar and Radhabai Savarkar in the village of Bhagur, near Nashik in Maharashtra. Political resentment against the British was always simmering just beneath the surface in Maharashtra, the heartland of the Maratha empire that the British had pushed aside to conquer India. The ancestors of the Savarkars had been mid-level officials in the Maratha administration and the memories were still fresh.[1]

Abhinav Bharat

Vinayak grew up against the backdrop of Vasudev Balwant Phadke's work to unite various communities in Maharashtra and the south against the British and also Tilak's writings in *Kesari*. The killing of Walter Rand by the Chapekar brothers and their subsequent hanging had a big impact on him. When his family moved to Nashik in 1899, he organized a small group of friends called 'Mitra Mela'. They met regularly to discuss political ideas in a small room, with portraits of their heroes lining the walls—Chhatrapati Shivaji, Nana Saheb, Rani Laxmibai of Jhansi, Tatya Tope, Vasudev Balwant Phadke.

These were difficult times for the Savarkars. Damodar had passed away and the family were forced to sell their property and even jewellery. It was under these strained circumstances that Vinayak received a proposal to marry Yamuna, the eldest daughter of a wealthy aristocrat, Bhaurao Chiplunkar. He was frank with Bhaurao about his family's financial situation as well as his interest in pursuing further studies. Bhaurao

---

[1] Vikram Sampath, *Savarkar: Echoes from a Forgotten Past*, Penguin India, 2019.

promised to provide money to support both his family and his education. Vinayak married Yamuna in 1901, when they were both still teenagers.

With support from his in-laws, Vinayak joined Ferguson College in Poona (now Pune) to pursue an undergraduate degree in arts. He set up a branch of the Mitra Mela in the college, which soon attracted a large number of students. A year later, Vinayak also began to attend classes in Deccan College for an LLB (Bachelor of Law), where he set up a Mitra Mela too. The Mitra Melas organized talks by prominent speakers of that time on a variety of subjects. They also published plays, poetry and essays, often with a nationalist tilt. The success of the Mitra Melas led to the establishment of branches in more colleges across Maharashtra, and Vinayak became a rising student leader.

In 1904, the Mitra Melas held a convention in Nashik that was attended by more than 200 delegates. At the event, Vinayak renamed the network Abhinav Bharat (New India or Young India). The choice of name was inspired directly by Mazzini's Young Italy. In front of a portrait of Chhatrapati Shivaji, a solemn oath was taken that began with:

> *Vande Mataram, in the name of God, in the name of Bharat Mata, in the name of all the martyrs who have shed their blood for Bharat Mata ...*'[2]

The following year, the Swadeshi movement erupted over the partition of Bengal. On Dussehra, 8 October, a large procession with cartloads of foreign-made clothes made its way through the streets of Poona. Vinayak led the procession and was joined midway by Tilak. A student named Vishnu

[2] *Ibid*

Ganesh Pingle, who would later play a role in the Ghadar movement, was also there. When they reached Lakdi Pul, speeches were delivered, and a huge bonfire was lit with all the clothes and other goods. The then principal of Ferguson College was not pleased when he heard that one of his brightest students was leading the Swadeshi boycotts. He expelled Savarkar from the hostel and fined him Rs 10. Tilak and several prominent Punekars spoke up for the student leader. Vinayak Savarkar was now a celebrity.

Savarkar finished his BA degree in December 1905 and moved to Bombay's Wilson College to finish the final year of his LLB. In the next few years, the Abhinav Bharat network spread across India. Vinayak's brother Babarao Savarkar and a hundred Abhinav Bharat members attended the troubled INC conference in Surat in 1907. Even as the two factions of the INC fought each other, Babarao and his team held a secret meeting with Aurobindo Ghosh and the Anushilan Samiti members from Bengal. They also scouted for young talent to spread their network to other states.

The Indian Sociologist

Shyamji Krishna Varma was born in Kachchh, Gujarat, in 1857. He lost his parents by the time he was ten, but generous relatives helped him pursue his education in Bombay. Around 1874, he met the religious and social reformer Dayanand Saraswati, and, a year later, became one of the first to be formally initiated into the Arya Samaj—a Hindu reform movement that advocated a return to simpler Vedic rites. The same year, he married Bhanumati, the daughter of a wealthy businessman.

Shyamji was academically gifted and his lectures on Sanskrit and Hinduism attracted a lot of attention. The Boden professor of Sanskrit at Oxford, Monier Williams, invited Shyamji to Oxford, where he soon became a well-known academic. He became a member of the prestigious Royal Asiatic Society in 1881. Shyamji also studied law and became a barrister by 1885. He then returned to India and was quite a favourite with the colonial administration, although he secretly harboured nationalist views. When he began to express some of these views, the British treated him with suspicion. Shyamji and Bhanumati decided to move to Europe in 1897.

Living between London and Paris, Shyamji discovered yet another talent—as an investor. He acquired a large fortune from stocks, which allowed him to pursue his ideas independently. In January 1905, he started an English monthly called *Indian Sociologist*, which advocated 'home rule' (i.e., independence), though it was careful not to be seen as supporting violence. He also established contacts with other revolutionary publications.

Shyamji also established a hostel for Indian students, called India House, in London. Britain had the world's best universities at the time, and he felt that talented nationalist Indians should be exposed to them. The hostel was inaugurated in July 1905 in the presence of Lala Lajpat Rai, Dadabhai Naoroji, Madame Bhikaji Cama and a handful of sympathetic British politicians.

Bhikaji Cama

BOMBAY
b. 24 September 1861
d. 13 August 1936, 74 years

Shyamji and his friend Sardar Sinh Ravaji Rana also instituted three scholarships named after Maharana Pratap of Mewar, Mughal Emperor Akbar and Chhatrapati Shivaji. Interestingly, the students who received the scholarships had to pledge that they would not join the British government service in India or elsewhere. The call for applications was published in *Indian Sociologist* in December 1905, and Savarkar applied for it. His application included a letter of recommendation from Tilak himself. He got the scholarship. Savarkar left Bombay for England aboard *SS Persia* in June 1906. He would not have been surprised to learn that a letter from the Special Crime Branch, Poona, was also on its way to the India Office Crime Branch in London, making it clear that Scotland Yard needed to keep an eye on a certain Vinayak Savarkar.

Duels with Scotland Yard

Savarkar was admitted to Gray's Inn in late July 1906 and began his legal studies. He also took up lodging at India House and almost immediately set up a branch of Abhinav Bharat. India House became a hive of revolutionary activity. In the next few months, Savarkar recruited an extraordinary group of young men who would leave a mark on India's struggle for Independence, including Lala Hardayal, Madanlal Dhingra, V.V.S. Aiyar, Virendranath Chattopadhyay (nicknamed 'Chatto'), Panduranga Bapat and Bhai Parmanand. Using Shyamji's contacts, he connected with a group in Paris, which included Bhikaji Cama and S.R. Rana.

The date 1 May 1907 marked the golden jubilee of the Revolt of 1857. It was observed in Britain by major events

REVOLUTIONARY	MADAME BHIKAJI CAMA	V.V.S. AIYAR	MADANLAL DHINGRA
BIRTH YEAR	1861	1881	1883
BIRTHPLACE	Bombay	Madras Presidency	Amritsar
PROFESSION	Social work, activism, writing; worked in London, Paris & other European cities	Law, practised in Rangoon and then London	Civil Engineering, studied at University College London
MUST-KNOW FACT	Cama unfurled a flag of free India at the International Socialist Congress in Stuttgart in 1907.	Though initially suspicious of Savarkar, Aiyar became his effective second-in-command.	Dhingra shot Sir William Curzon Wyllie, the officer who blocked Savarkar's admission to the Bar at Gray's Inn.

commemorating the heroism and sacrifices of British officers and soldiers. In plays, articles and editorials, the Indian rebels were presented as marauders and bandits. *The Daily Telegraph* ran a headline a few days later: 'Fifty Years Ago, This Week, an Empire Saved by Deeds of Heroism.'

No Indian dared to openly challenge this narrative, except the Abhinav Bharat group at India House. As historian Vikram Sampath puts it, 'It is noteworthy that no political party or groups back in India organized any commemoration of such an important milestone of the nation's past and the task was left to a few young students in distant London.'[3] More than 200 people attended the event at India House. In a moving speech, Savarkar argued that 1857 was not a

[3] Vikram Sampath, *Savarkar: Echoes from a Forgotten Past,* Penguin India, 2019.

mere 'mutiny' but the 'First War of Indian Independence'—a rehearsal for a revolution that would overthrow the empire.

Given such open calls for rebellion, it was not surprising that Scotland Yard kept a close watch on India House by sending detectives in plain clothes. The students were aware of this, as they could see random men loitering outside. The detectives would sometimes follow an individual around the city. The students took to mocking them by asking them for directions or speaking to them in familiar terms. This immensely annoyed the policemen. Savarkar also mastered the art of giving them the slip. He would walk along the road until he saw a free taxi coming and he would suddenly jump in. The detectives would have to wait until another taxi came along, by which time Savarkar had already made his getaway.

Scotland Yard next decided to place a couple of moles inside India House. One of them was Kirtikar, who claimed to have come to London to study dentistry. He soon befriended Savarkar. It quickly became clear that he had very little interest in dentistry, so Savarkar and Aiyar decided to find out a bit more about the student. They first found out that he had not attended any classes after his first week. So when Kirtikar was away one evening, Aiyar entered his room using a master key and discovered a copy of his report to Scotland Yard. When Kirtikar returned, Aiyar held a revolver to his head and made him confess. After some discussion with the others, Savarkar decided to let Kirtikar stay at India House on the condition that the students would first read and edit his reports. One can imagine them sitting around the dinner table late at night, amusing themselves by inserting deliberately inaccurate information into the reports.

The 1857 Book

One of the things Savarkar realized while in London was that the British were systematically rewriting Indian history in a way that bolstered their rule in India and reinforced the myth of white supremacy. A prime example of this manipulation was the narrative around the events of 1857, which tarred Indians as the villains. Savarkar decided to rectify this. In the author's note to his book *The Indian War of Independence of 1857* (originally written in Marathi), he stated, 'A nation that has no consciousness of its past has no future.'[4] Savarkar wrote passionately about how Hindus and Muslims had risen up together against oppression by a foreign invader. Importantly, he again mentioned clearly that 1857 was just the 'great rehearsal' and that 'there slumbers a volcano under that surface.'[5]

As the book neared completion, Scotland Yard received one of its chapters from a mole at India House. Savarkar noticed the missing chapter and quickly completed the manuscript. Then a copy was sent secretly to Babarao for printing in India. By this time, Scotland Yard had realized what was going on and the full network of British intelligence was alerted. The

---

[4] Vinayak Savarkar, *The Indian War of Independence of 1857*, 1909 (online digital copy from Columbia University Library).
[5] *Ibid.*

viceroy, Lord Minto, heard about the book and issued strict orders for it to not be allowed into India. Of course, the book was already in India, but Babarao was unable to find a printer willing to publish it. He was forced to send the manuscript to France and then to Germany, where a growing interest in Sanskrit meant that a couple of printers were at least familiar with the Devanagari script. However, they were not familiar with the Marathi language and did a shoddy job of printing the book.

Back in London, Aiyar translated the book into English with the help of Marathi-speaking members of Abhinav Bharat. Again, the manuscript was sent to France and Germany for printing, but no one wanted to print it for fear of offending the British. Eventually, a small printer in Holland agreed. Copies were then smuggled into India wrapped in the innocuous covers of books such as *Don Quixote* and *The Posthumous Papers of the Pickwick Club*. One box of such books was smuggled in by Sikandar Hayat Khan. Simultaneously, copies were sold to the Indian diaspora across the world—in Paris, London and all over the United States. The book was not banned in Britain and was circulated widely in the Indian student community.

The book was an instant hit and would become almost required reading for those supporting a revolutionary path to Indian Independence. Bhikaji got a second edition printed in France and translated it into French. A few years later, a third edition was printed in the United States by Lala Hardayal and sold openly. In the late 1920s, Bhagat Singh secretly printed another edition in India. Yet another edition was later printed by Rashbehari Bose in Japan. The book would have a big influence on generations of revolutionaries.

An Evening at the Imperial Institute

It was not just Scotland Yard that knew about the revolutionaries at India House. Revolutionaries in Europe were aware of it, and many well-known activists visited the hostel and met Savarkar and other Abhinav Bharat members. This included Irish nationalists and Russian communists.

A well-known personality who visited India House was Mohandas Karamchand Gandhi. There is an eyewitness account that the first meeting between the stalwarts did not go well. Savarkar was cooking prawns and invited Gandhi to join his group for a meal. Gandhi refused as he was a strict vegetarian and Savarkar is said to have retorted, 'Well, if you cannot eat with us, how on earth are you going to work with us?'[6]

The friction between the two was more than just a personality clash, or even a difference of opinion about the use of violence. The revolutionaries were very suspicious of Gandhi from the beginning. *Indian Sociologist* had been severely critical of Gandhi's open support of the British against the Zulus during the Bambatha Rebellion of 1906 in South Africa. Thousands of Zulus would be massacred. These suspicions were reinforced by Gandhi's active recruitment of Indian soldiers for the British cause during the First World War.

In early 1909, the revolutionary network began to ramp up its activities. Sikandar Hayat Khan and Mirza Abbas procured twenty Browning pistols and a large cache of ammunition from Paris. These were packed into a false-bottomed box and taken to Bombay by Chaturbhuj Amin, the chef at India House. Amin successfully delivered the pistols

---
[6] Vikram Sampath, *Savarkar: Echoes from a Forgotten Past*, Penguin India, 2019.

to the Abhinav Bharat group in Maharashtra. Unfortunately, the police found out about this and raided Babarao's house in Nashik. Although they did not find the pistols, they found a copy of the Russian bomb manual that Hemchandra Das and Pandurang Bapat had acquired in Paris. The police were already aware of the manual, as it had been found in Barin Ghosh's Maniktola garden house.

Savarkar heard of Babarao's arrest around the same time that he heard that his son Prabhakar had died of smallpox. It was a difficult time for the Savarkar family. The London press was full of stories about the activities at India House and Savarkar's admission to the Bar at Gray's Inn was indefinitely postponed for obviously political reasons. The key person who had blocked his admission was Sir William Curzon Wyllie, a former officer of the British Indian Army who now served as aide-de-camp to Lord George Hamilton, the secretary of state for India. Part of his role was keeping an eye on Indians in London, whether visiting princes or students. He would occasionally invite members of the community, including those from India House, for a friendly meal and pump them for information. It was he who had created a file on Savarkar and passed it on to Gray's Inn.

The National Indian Association held one of its regular evening parties on 1 July 1909 at the Imperial Institute in South Kensington. The idea was to encourage interaction between Indians and the British elite. Madanlal Dhingra arrived punctually and chatted with many guests. It was quite late in the evening when William Curzon Wyllie turned up. As he walked around exchanging pleasantries with students, he stopped for a conversation with Dhingra. All of a sudden, Dhingra pulled out a small Colt and shot him point-blank four times. There was pandemonium in the room even as Dhingra turned the gun on himself, but was overpowered. His glasses had fallen off in the scuffle and, unfazed, he told his captors, 'Wait, let me just put my spectacles on!'

The assassination drew a lot of condemnation from the British as well as prominent Indians. Dhingra's family publicly disowned him and Gopal Krishna Gokhale stated that his act had 'blackened the Indian name'. Gandhi wrote a stinging article criticizing Dhingra. On 5 July, the Indian community of London congregated at Caxton Hall under the chairmanship of the Aga Khan to discuss how they could 'rehabilitate themselves among their fellow-subjects of the Empire'.[7] A resolution expressing 'horror and indignation' was put to the vote. It was expected to be unanimously adopted, when a young man jumped up and screamed, 'No! Not Unanimously!' It was Savarkar, who had turned up to defend his friend. He was immediately attacked and punched. Even then, Savarkar stood up on a chair and announced that he would oppose the resolution until the last drop of his blood. He and Aiyar were then thrown out of the hall.

Dhingra's trial began a few days later. The prosecution put forward a heap of evidence and a large number of witnesses. Dhingra stood silently through it all. When the judge finally asked him if he wished to defend himself, Dhingra said that he merely wanted to read out a statement:

I do not wish to say anything in defence of myself, but simply to prove the justice of my deed. As for myself, no English court of law has any authority to arrest and detain me in prison, or pass sentence of death on me. That is the reason I do not have any counsel to defend me. And I maintain that if it is patriotic in an

---

[7] As quoted in Vikram Sampath, *Savarkar: Echoes from a Forgotten Past*, Penguin India, 2019.

> *Englishman to fight against the Germans if they were to occupy this country, it is much more justifiable in my case to fight against the English. I hold the English people responsible for the murder of 80 millions of the Indian people ... Just as the Germans have no right to occupy this country, the English people have no right to occupy India ...*[8]

The courtroom heard this in a hushed silence before the judge pronounced him guilty and sentenced him to death by hanging. With Dhingra's family having disowned him, Savarkar was the only one who went to meet him in prison. It was an emotional meeting, where Dhingra revealed that his final wish was to be cremated in accordance with Hindu rites.

On the morning of 17 August 1909, at the stroke of nine, Dhingra was hanged. He was twenty-five, and is said to have embraced martyrdom with a smile. Leading British politicians such as Winston Churchill and Lloyd George privately expressed their admiration for

[8] Ibid.

him. His body was not handed over for a Hindu cremation as per his last wish, but was buried inside the jail. Dhingra's remains were brought back to India in December 1976. A statue in his memory stands in his hometown, Amritsar, at one end of a road that leads to Jallianwala Bagh.

SS Morea

One predictable outcome of the Wyllie assassination was that India House was closed down. At the last meeting of Abhinav Bharat at the venue, Savarkar made an impassioned speech in Dhingra's memory. However, he and his associates were now homeless. With Scotland Yard keeping a close watch on their movements, Savarkar was forced to share a dingy room in a London slum. Meanwhile, his health deteriorated.

Back in India, the Abhinav Bharat network had ramped up attacks on colonial officials. Two bombs were thrown at the viceroy's procession in November 1909 when he and Lady Minto were making their way from Ahmedabad station towards Raipur Gate.[9] The bombs failed to explode but the message was clear—even the senior-most British officials were no longer safe. The accused, Mohanlal Pandya, was linked to both Barin Ghosh's Anushilan Samiti and to Abhinav Bharat.

Just a few weeks later, another young member of Abhinav Bharat—Anantrao Laxman Kanhere—assassinated Arthur Jackson, the district collector of Nashik. Jackson had not only arrested Babarao, but had paraded him handcuffed through the streets of Nashik to intimidate the population. Unsurprisingly, the police saw the Savarkar family at the heart of these developments. Vinayak's younger brother

---

[9] *'Vile Attack on Lord & Lady Minto'*, Press Association report, Calcutta, 15 November 1909 (National Library of New Zealand, online digital library, https://paperspast.natlib.govt.nz/newspapers/ESD19091116.2.49).

Narayanrao was arrested as part of the investigations and subjected to severe torture in prison.

With both his brothers in police custody, it was obvious to Savarkar that he was next. In early January 1910, he shifted to Paris, where he was welcomed by S.R. Rana and Bhikaji Cama. Over the next few months, Savarkar published several fiery articles and wrote a new book titled *History of the Sikhs*. Three copies of the manuscript were made, but with surveillance heightened, the book was never printed. The manuscript has been lost and we only know about it from references in Savarkar's memoirs.

In Paris, Savarkar's health got better. However, the colonial government in India wanted him extradited and made out a prima facie case against him. A warrant was issued against him in London and he was declared a fugitive. The British wanted to try Savarkar in India, where they could use draconian laws and stacked courts, whereas in England he would have gotten away with a light sentence.

Despite being fully aware of the situation, Savarkar decided to return to London in March 1910. Shyamji and the others warned him against it, but he was insistent. It is not clear why he made this decision, given the obvious dangers, but it is likely that he felt guilty of living in relative comfort in Paris while many of his followers were facing arrest in London. As soon as he got off the train at Victoria Station, he was arrested and taken to the Bow Street police station.

Savarkar was sent to Brixton Prison while the formalities of his extradition to India were worked out. Even as the court hearings were taking place, Irish revolutionaries of Sinn Fein decided to rescue him. They had noticed that Savarkar was taken to court in a certain cab and decided to waylay it before making a getaway by car. On the appointed day, the Irish team did stop the cab but discovered that it only contained the detectives, not Savarkar. Evidently, British intelligence had received a tip-off and had sent Savarkar by a different vehicle. Thus, what may have been a very dramatic escape was averted. Winston Churchill, then secretary of state for home affairs, signed the extradition order in June 1910.

Under heavy security, Savarkar was put on board the Peninsular and Oriental liner *SS Morea* on 1 July. Two British police officers, an Indian police officer and two Indian head constables were on the ship to keep an eye on the revolutionary.

SS Morea made a scheduled two-day stop at Marseilles on 7 and 8 July. The police officers were aware of the Indian revolutionary groups operating in France and were edgy. They kept him in their line of sight for all of the first day and even ensured that he had his evening bath in a bathroom that did not have a porthole. Next morning, however, Savarkar made an unusual request—to use the lavatory at 6.15 a.m. One of the British officers sleepily took him to the nearest toilet and left him with the two constables. They did not pay attention to the fact that it had a porthole.

Savarkar immediately opened the porthole and began to squeeze himself out. When he was halfway out, one of the constables looked into the toilet through a crack and realized what was happening. The two tried to break down the door but it was locked solid. They raised the alarm. By now Savarkar had managed to jump off and swim to the quay. He began to run towards the town to look for the getaway car that was supposed to be waiting for him. Sadly it was not there. An exhausted Savarkar could run no further, and his pursuers were closing in. Meanwhile, Brigadier Pesque of the French Gendarmerie Maritime arrived and arrested him. Savarkar desperately tried to explain to him that he was a political prisoner seeking asylum in France, but the Frenchman did not understand English and promptly handed him back to the party from *SS Morea*.

The getaway car with Bhikaji Cama, Aiyar and Chatto arrived just moments after Savarkar had been handed back. Madame Cama raised the issue of allowing foreign officials to drag away a political refugee from French soil as an insult to French sovereignty. It became a cause célèbre in the French press and the French ambassador to Britain demanded that Savarkar be handed back to France. The issue was hotly debated in the French Chamber of Deputies. With diplomatic temperatures rising, the matter was sent for arbitration to the international tribunal at The Hague. Savarkar was now an internationally recognized figure and his case attracted a lot of attention not just in India and Britain, but all over Europe.

The colonial administration in India, meanwhile, had fast-tracked Savarkar's trial by a special tribunal in Bombay. His fiery speeches and articles were presented against him, and he was also accused of sending the cache of Browning pistols used in the Nashik assassination. His lawyers tried to delay the proceedings by arguing that the international arbitration should be settled first, but were overruled. On 30 January 1911, the special tribunal ruled that Vinayak Savarkar was guilty of abetment to murder and sentenced him to double transportation for life—i.e., fifty years of incarceration at the dreaded Cellular Jail in the Andamans.

Everything now depended on the outcome at The Hague. The French argued their case strongly, but on

24 February, the case was decided in Britain's favour. At the jail, the jailors forced Savarkar to wear an iron plaque around his neck at all times, with '1960' written on it, meant to remind him of the year he would be released. When the superintendent saw Savarkar's sad expression, he mocked him, 'Don't worry, His Majesty's benign government will release you in 1960 for sure.' Savarkar replied, 'Death is kinder, it may release me earlier!' Then they both laughed.[10]

[10] Vikram Sampath, *Savarkar: Echoes from a Forgotten Past*, Penguin India, 2019.

◆ 4 ◆
THE GHADAR

THE CONSTANT ATTACKS and the visible spread of revolutionary ideas among the youth finally convinced the colonial authorities that some concessions had to be made to the Indians. These came in the form of the Indian Councils Act introduced in November 1909 (commonly known as the Morley-Minto Reforms). It provided for somewhat greater representation of Indians through elected members in legislative councils.

It was widely recognized at that time that the changes had been forced by the revolutionaries. Even Gandhi acknowledged this in an interview at the time: 'England is, I believe, easily influenced by the use of gunpowder.'[1] Thus, it is fair to say that the first generation of revolutionary leaders had achieved quite a lot within a decade but they had still not threatened the foundations of the colonial edifice. That changed with the arrival of the second generation of revolutionary leaders. Enter Rashbehari Bose.

Chandni Chowk 1912

Rashbehari was born in a remote village in Bengal in 1886 but grew up in his maternal uncle's house in the French enclave of Chandernagore. The enclave was a hotbed of revolutionary activity and a teenage Rashbehari was exposed to the activities of the Anushilan Samiti. He was particularly influenced by the ideas of Swami Vivekananda and Aurobindo Ghosh. His father, Binod Behari Bose, was a clerk at a government press in Shimla and he arranged for his son to work as a copy editor at the press. Rashbehari did

---
[1] As quoted in Vikram Sampath, *Savarkar: Echoes from a Forgotten Past*, Penguin India, 2019.

not like the job, but used the opportunity to hone his English-language skills.

In 1906, Rashbehari got a job as a laboratory assistant at the Forest Research Institute (FRI) in Dehradun. While there, he made friends with Jitendra Mohan Chatterjee from Saharanpur.[2] Chatterjee was part of a network of revolutionaries in Punjab and the United Provinces (now roughly Uttar Pradesh). The Punjab group was led by Sardar Ajit Singh, and included his brother Kishan Singh (Bhagat Singh's father), and Sufi Amba Prasad. They were in touch with Savarkar's group in London through Hardayal, who was then studying at Oxford. Similarly, there was a group in Delhi led by Amir Chand, a schoolmaster. Rashbehari came to know some of these individuals.

In 1907, the colonial administration decided to crack down on nationalists in Punjab, and sent both Lala Lajpat Rai and Ajit Singh to prison in Mandalay, Burma (now Myanmar). Realizing that he had been compromised, Jitendra Mohan Chatterjee summoned Rashbehari and gave him a detailed overview of the existing revolutionary network before leaving the country. Rashbehari was now the only one who understood the linkages between various groups in north-western India. Thus, a Bengali laboratory assistant in Dehradun became the nerve centre of revolutionary activity.

Rashbehari made a couple of trips to Chandernagore in 1911. During this time, he became closely acquainted with Moti Lal Roy, a close associate of Aurobindo Ghosh, and was deeply influenced by the latter's religious views.[3] He also began to study the Bhagawad Gita. Rashbehari mooted the idea of carrying out a major strike against the British. The plan was to assassinate Viceroy Hardinge when he entered

---

[2] Uma Mukherjee, *Two Great Revolutionaries*, Dey's Publishing, 1966 (reprinted 2004).
[3] Takeshi Nakajima, *Bose of Nakamuraya: An Indian Revolutionary in Japan*, translated from Japanese by Prem Motwani, Promilla & Co, 2005.

Delhi in a grand viceregal procession in December 1912 to mark the shift of the capital from Calcutta to Delhi. Bose asked for an accomplice to help him, and the Anushilan Samiti chose Basanta Kumar Biswas.

The date of the viceregal procession was 23 December 1912, and the revolutionary team assembled in Amir Chand's house in Delhi two days earlier. The ceremonial entry into Delhi (what we now know as Old Delhi) was a pompous affair, with horses and elephants, intended to impress the Indians. It was to make its way through Chandni Chowk to the Red Fort, reminiscent of Mughal-era processions. On the morning of 23 December, Rashbehari and Biswas (dressed as a woman) positioned themselves at Chandni Chowk's Katra Dhulia wholesale cloth market.

Around 11.45 a.m., the procession reached Katra Dhulia. Lord Hardinge and his wife were on the third elephant, and Biswas accurately threw the bomb. The explosion killed an attendant and severely injured the viceroy. In the ensuing commotion, Rashbehari and Biswas escaped. Biswas took a train to Lahore and Rashbehari to Dehradun.

The incident shook the empire. The revolutionaries had nearly killed the viceroy at an event meant as a display of British power. Rashbehari, meanwhile, carried on with his duties at FRI as if nothing had happened. He organized a meeting to condemn the attack on Hardinge and was so convincing that when Hardinge visited Dehradun a few months later, he was put in charge of the welcome committee!

This changed after Biswas carried out a second attack in May 1913 on a British official in Lahore. This time Biswas lost his nerve and the bomb killed a passer-by. Although Biswas escaped from the venue, the police quickly realized that the

picric acid bomb was exactly the same design as the one thrown in Chandni Chowk. A huge operation was launched to hunt down the suspects. The net began to close around the group, and eventually several members were arrested. Biswas was arrested when, against Rashbehari's advice, he went back to Bengal to attend his father's funeral. It was his uncle who informed the police. Biswas, Amir Chand, Avadh Behari and Bal Mukund were hanged for their involvement in the attacks.

The colonial government now gave itself draconian powers under the Indian Criminal Law Amendment Act and the Defence of India Act. There was a public outcry but the Loyalists who dominated the new legislative assembly put up little resistance. When Hardinge asked Gokhale what he would do if all the British officials one day just decided to go home, the latter replied that he would telegraph them before they reached Aden to come back![4]

In August 1913, Rashbehari shifted to Chandernagore. It was around this time that he reconnected with Sachindra Nath Sanyal of Varanasi as well as Jyotindra Nath Mukherjee (popularly known as Bagha Jatin). A few days later, Rashbehari, Bagha Jatin and another prominent revolutionary, Amarendra Nath Chatterjee, met secretly in the Panchavati garden in Dakhshineshwar. Here the revolutionaries decided that the time had come to organize a mass rebellion modelled on the Revolt of 1857. They also reached out to Aurobindo Ghosh in Pondicherry and received his blessings.[5]

Sachindra Nath Sanyal, or Sachin Sanyal, was born in 1893 into a Bengali family in Varanasi. His grandfather and great-grandfather were renowned Vedic scholars. The Sanyals were originally from Belur in Bengal and had been close to Rani Rashmoni. Having settled in Varanasi's Madanpura area, they intermarried with other Bengali families such as the Lahiris, who had settled in the neighbourhood. Thus, in three generations, the Sanyal-Lahiri clan came to have a web of family and friends in this part of Varanasi. The revolutionaries would soon exploit this labyrinth.

Sachin Sanyal's ancestors had watched with concern the political, economic and cultural domination of India by the British. This had elicited many responses, ranging from that

---

[4] *Struggle for Freedom*, edited by R.C. Majumdar, Bharatiya Vidya Bhawan, 1969 (reprinted in 1978).
[5] Uma Mukherjee, *Two Great Revolutionaries*, Dey's Publishing, 1966 (reprinted in 2004).

of the Westernizing Brahmos to that of the orthodox. The Sanyal–Lahiri clan were part of a third response—that of modernizing revivalists who agreed with the Brahmos on the need for social and educational modernization but did not wish to compromise on cultural traditions. Thus, they were quick to embrace the English language and, in 1853, built the city's first 'modern' school called Bengali Tola Intercollege (it still exists). At the same time, the family was also invested in promoting and spreading Indic ideas. Sachin Sanyal's granduncle Shyama Charan Lahiri, popularly known as Lahiri Mahashaya, is still revered for giving kriya yoga its modern form and spreading its practice widely.[6]

Sachin Sanyal founded a branch of the Anushilan Samiti in Varanasi in 1908. The akhada had a small open area with a few trees, a platform and a room.[7] Young men gathered there to practise wrestling, boxing, the use of daggers and so on. The room had a small library that contained religious and revolutionary literature, and there were regular lectures on the Bhagawad Gita, Indian history and international revolutionaries such as Garibaldi. Following the arrest of Anushilan Samiti members in Bengal, Sanyal changed the name of the group to Young Men's Association to stay under the radar.

Sanyal and Rashbehari had first met in 1911 or 1912, but it was really in 1913 that he became Rashbehari's chief lieutenant and co-conspirator. By then, Rashbehari had realized that the police would eventually locate him in the French enclave. He decided to shift his base to Varanasi, where the Sanyal clan could hide him. It was in the winding lanes of Bengali Tola, Madanpura, that Rashbehari and Sanyal began to put together a plan for a large-scale revolt in the British Indian

---

[6] Dr Ashok Kumar Chatterjee, *Purana Purusha: Yogiraj Sri Shama Churn Lahiree: A Complete Biography*, Yogiraj Publications, 1981 (reprinted in 2014).
[7] 'Reminiscences of Shri J.N. Mukherjee, J.N. Sanyal and Others', Commemorative brochure for the 90th year of Sachindra Nath Sanyal, 1983.

Army. A steady stream of trusted revolutionaries visited the effective headquarters in Sanyal's ancestral home, including Vishnu Ganesh Pingle from Poona, Pratul Chandra Ganguli from Dacca (now Dhaka) and Bagha Jatin.

The Sikhs in North America

Following the death of Maharaja Ranjit Singh in 1839, his kingdom quickly descended into turmoil. Defeats in the First Anglo-Sikh War of 1845-46 and in the Second Anglo-Sikh War of 1848-49 resulted in the East India Company occupying Punjab. Despite fresh memories of a bitter war, the Sikhs remained loyal to the British cause during the Revolt of 1857. Therefore, the colonial administration decided that the Sikh elite, and more generally the Punjabi elite, could be useful native allies.

As part of this strategy, the British invested systematically in a Sikh identity, which was distinct from its Hindu roots. Just like a section of the Bengali elite was won over through favourable access to Western education and government jobs, the Punjabi elite was given favourable enrolment in the army, titles, government contracts and land grants in canal-irrigated areas.

Meanwhile, the wider population rapidly became pauperized. Six famines ravaged Punjab in the first fifty years of British rule. The simmering resentments led to the Kuka Rebellion of 1872 by Namdhari Sikhs. It was quickly crushed but socio-economic conditions worsened. Government records show that 3 million people perished in the province from epidemics between 1897 and 1918.[8] In the first decade of the twentieth century, inspired by Tilak's efforts in

[8] Harish K. Puri, *Ghadar Movement: A Short History*, National Book Trust, 2011.

Maharashtra, Ajit Singh formed the Bharat Mata Society and began to mobilize the peasantry. Recognizing the threat, the colonial authorities deported Lala Lajpat Rai and Ajit Singh to Mandalay in 1907.

The feeling of discontent spread to a growing diaspora in North America. The Canadian government suddenly woke up to the possibility that a growing Indian population could permanently settle in British Columbia. Blatantly racist laws were introduced to stem the inflow. Former soldiers of the British Indian Army felt particularly insulted by an empire for which they had risked their lives in various colonial wars. They began to organize themselves through a network of gurudwaras. Since many of them came from villages in Punjab that had been part of Ajit Singh's movement, they were already familiar with the ideas of the revolutionaries.

Their efforts at mobilization were given a boost in 1907 by the arrival of Harnam Singh Sahri and Taraknath Das. Taraknath Das was an active member of the Dacca Anushilan Samiti and had escaped to the United States to study, before making his way to Vancouver. Taraknath was soon involved in organizing protests against racist laws targeting Indians. He also began to publish a periodical named *Free Hindustan* on the same lines as Shyamji's *Indian Sociologist*. Harnam Singh, like Ajit Singh, was a Sikh involved in the Arya Samaj movement. He began to publish a Punjabi monthly in Gurmukhi script named *Swadesh Sewak* (Servant of the Motherland).

The British intelligence network in both India and Canada was aware of what was happening and decided to contain it. The job was given to one William Hopkinson, who was proficient in both Hindi and Punjabi. His brief was to infiltrate the Indian community, particularly the gurudwaras, to gather information and subvert any anti-British movement from inside.

The first target was Taraknath, who had been publishing articles exhorting Sikh troops to rise up against the British. He was expelled from Canada. Meanwhile, the Punjabi community in British Columbia formed two organizations—the United India League and the Khalsa Diwan Society. The former was more concerned with socio-political issues of the wider Indian community while the latter focused specifically on Sikh religious issues.

Hopkinson saw the establishment of these organizations as a major threat and informed his superiors. He was soon provided significant resources to penetrate the gurudwaras to provide support to pro-British groups within the Sikhs as well as cause internal divisions. Meanwhile, the Canadian authorities continued to make immigration ever more difficult for Indians. Given the increasingly hostile treatment, many Indians decided to leave Canada and move down the coast to the United States. Thus, California became a hub of anti-British sentiment. This was when Hardayal arrived in San Francisco.

Yugantar Ashram

Lala Hardayal was born in 1884 in Delhi. He earned a bachelor's degree in Sanskrit from St Stephen's College before doing a master's from Punjab University, Lahore. During his time in Lahore, he met Lala Lajpat Rai and Bhai Parmanand, who drew him into the Arya Samaj fold.

In 1905, Hardayal won a scholarship to study history in London and, in 1907, became a Boden scholar at St John's

College, Oxford. Like many contemporary Indian students in Britain, Hardayal was deeply influenced by Savarkar's lectures at India House. He soon became an active member of Abhinav Bharat. When he returned briefly to India in 1908, he already had a reputation as a revolutionary thinker. He met several nationalist leaders of north India, including Lala Lajpat Rai, who had just returned from Mandalay. A few months later, Lajpat Rai received a tip-off that the government was planning to arrest Hardayal, and he was forced to leave the country.

Hardayal moved to Paris, where he and Madam Cama published a revolutionary paper, *Bande Mataram,* named after the periodical edited by Aurobindo Ghosh. However, after failing to rescue Savarkar in Marseilles, Hardayal began to feel restless. In 1911, he moved to California. Fame of his scholarship soon spread and he was invited to deliver lectures at Stanford on philosophy, Sanskrit and Indian history. He also became the focus of the Indian student community on the West Coast. An informal group called Nalanda Club was set up in a rented apartment in Berkeley and members would meet regularly to discuss India-related issues.

By 1912, Hardayal's network started to spread to the migrant worker community due to the efforts of Sohan Singh Bhakna, who had built a network among Punjabi migrants in Portland, Oregon. A large number would gather to hear Hardayal when he visited Portland in March 1913. Soon, a formal association headed by Bhakna and Hardayal was established. It was headquartered at a rented house in 436 Hill Street, San Francisco. The house, named Yugantar Ashram after Barin Ghosh's revolutionary paper *Jugantar,* served as a gathering place, printing house and accommodation for a small group of volunteers.

The most important function of the ashram was the publication of a weekly called *The Ghadar* (The Uprising). Published in Urdu and Punjabi, the paper was announced on 1 November 1913 as: 'Today there begins in foreign lands, but in the language of the country, a war against English rule.' The top of the front page was inscribed with *'Bande Mataram'* and *'Angrezi Raj ka Dushman* (Enemy of the British Rule)'.

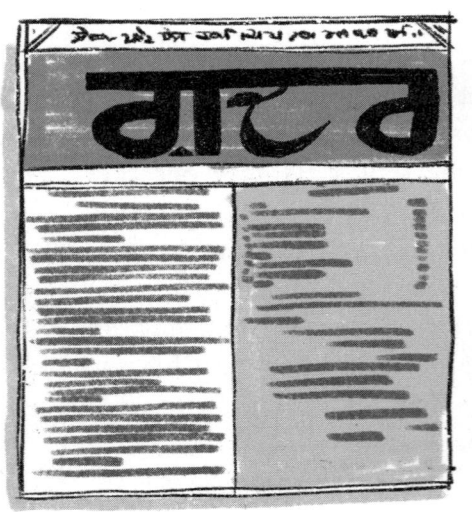

The paper contained news, opinion pieces, patriotic verses, bits of history and updates on armed revolts in other colonized countries such as Ireland. It rapidly became popular and was soon circulated by post and by hand in faraway places such as Trinidad, Singapore, Manila and Malaya (now Malaysia). The network of Sikh gurudwaras played an important role in disseminating the paper. In fact, the public singing of some of the verses became a regular feature in many gurudwaras.

The British authorities were aware of the new paper and its dangerous contents, thanks to Hopkinson's intelligence reports. The entry of the weekly was banned under the Sea Customs Act. On 30 January 1914, 215 bundles of *The Ghadar* were intercepted at the Bombay port. The British also began to put pressure on the United States to curb the activities of Hardayal. On 24 March, Hardayal was served a warrant of arrest. Since he was guaranteed freedom of expression under the US Constitution, he was accused of spreading anarchism through one of his speeches. He was soon released on bail and escaped to Berlin. Ram Chandra Peshawari, an old associate of Amir Chand, succeeded Hardayal as the chief editor of *The Ghadar*.

If anything, the attempt to arrest Hardayal had increased popular interest in the weekly and its associated movement, now identified as the Ghadar Party and the Ghadarites. As Europe began to lurch towards a war in mid-1914, Bhakna decided that the time had come for the Ghadarites to move back to India to participate in the coming revolution.

The February Plan

Even as groups of Ghadarite Sikhs were moving back to India, Sachindra Nath Sanyal and Rashbehari Bose were hard at work in Varanasi. A constant flow of trusted revolutionaries reported the latest developments and went out with instructions. Rashbehari's old network in Punjab meant that he was in touch with sympathizers in the province, including the returning Ghadarites. Rashbehari sent Sanyal to Punjab so he could speak to various groups and also sound out some of the army regiments. The declaration of war in July 1914 appeared as a godsend. Here was an opportunity to rake up trouble while the British were busy diverting their troops to the battlefields, and at the same time recruit and arm new Indian regiments.

In his famous book *Bandi Jeevan* (A Life in Prison), Sanyal describes how he crisscrossed north-western India, secretly meeting revolutionary groups and sympathetic soldiers from different army regiments.[9] The meetings were sometimes in the barracks and sometimes in a secluded grove near the railway station—always nervous gatherings, despite the patriotic zeal. Secrecy was critical, but concealing a plan involving so many people was no easy task. Many of the Ghadarites, especially those returning from North America, were pumped up and would get into unnecessary fights with the authorities. Such incidents meant that Sanyal and Rashbehari had to be very careful about whom they involved in their planning. They needed a trusted point person operating in the Lahore–Amritsar area, and decided on Kartar Singh Saraba, who had been Hardayal's assistant at Yugantar Ashram. He was barely eighteen and had only recently returned from California, but he proved to be an energetic organizer.

Similar networks were also being activated in the United Provinces. Vishnu Ganesh Pingle was sent to work on the barracks in Meerut. Sanyal was already in touch with regiments in and around Varanasi. However, Bengal was more complicated. The movement had widespread support in the province, but with the arrest of Aurobindo and Barin Ghosh, it had split into several small groups.

[9] Sachindra Nath Sanyal, *Bandi Jeevan*, reprinted in Hindi by Sakshi Prakashan, 2015.

Sanyal and Rashbehari eventually opted to work with a group led by Bagha Jatin. He had brought together surviving fragments of Barin's original team. It would, therefore, come to be known as the Jugantar group, after Barin's paper. It was disciplined and, unlike the others, invested in preparing for large-scale operations rather than just isolated attacks. Bagha Jatin had built up a working relationship with the Anushilan Samiti branches in Dacca and Chandernagore. Therefore, the Jugantar group was given the task of coordinating the revolution in eastern India.

In July 1914, war broke out in Europe. It was clear from the beginning that the British would not only have to divert military resources from India but also be forced to make fresh recruitments. This was the opportunity that the revolutionaries had been waiting for. From across India they visited Rashbehari and Sanyal in Varanasi and went back to organize local units in preparation of the coming revolt. None of them would have noticed a teenager named Subhas Chandra Bose, who was also in the city at that time on a spiritual quest. The paths of the two Boses would meet decades later during the Second World War.

The British intelligence services were aware by now that something was afoot. They began to arrest and question Sikhs returning from North America. Rashbehari and Sanyal realized that they could not delay things too much in the face of such pressure on the Punjabis. They also received information that some of the primed regiments in north-west India would leave to participate in the war in March 1915. During a clandestine meeting after dusk on a boat in the middle of the Ganga, Rashbehari told the representative from Bengal that the Jugantar group should get ready to coordinate attacks on the police and treasury establishments across Bengal. A few weeks later, he left for Punjab, where he took charge of arrangements with Mula Singh as his right-hand man. Sanyal stayed back in Varanasi to coordinate operations in the United Provinces.

The date for the revolt was fixed for 21 February 1915. The plan was that the first uprising would take place at Mian Mir cantonment, Lahore. This would be the signal for simultaneous revolts in Rawalpindi and Ferozepore. This would be followed by the regiments in Jubbalpore, Varanasi and so on. The Bengal revolutionaries would then start their attacks and try to take over Dacca.

On 13 February, the conspirators had a setback when Mula Singh was arrested. At the same time, a British intelligence mole, Kirpal Singh, managed to get into the inner circle. Suspicions were aroused when he was seen on 15 February speaking to a police officer at Lahore station. Rashbehari responded by bringing the date of the revolt forward to 19 February, but was unable to neutralize Kirpal Singh, who found out about the new date and again informed the authorities. Just hours before the revolt was supposed to be triggered, the police carried out several raids in Lahore on suspected hideouts. The army was put on high alert across the province and all Indian guards were replaced by Europeans at arms depots and key installations.

Once it became obvious that the British officers were fully aware of the plan, the Indian soldiers in the regiments in Punjab decided it was foolhardy to revolt. Kartar Singh Saraba arrived in the evening at the Ferozepore military camp with seventy lightly armed revolutionaries, but found that the British officers had already been alerted and taken preemptive action. Without any uprising in the north-west, the rolling wave of rebellion simply did not take off.

The only place where an uprising occurred in mid-February 1915 was in faraway Singapore. Although Rashbehari and Sanyal were not directly in touch with the regiments there, they were in contact with the wider Ghadarite network and would have been aware of the murmurings. The mutineers shot dead several British officers and took control of the city. It took three days of fighting before naval marines were able to recapture Singapore. Many of the rebel soldiers were lined up and publicly executed by a firing squad.

The lieutenant governor of Punjab, Michael O'Dwyer, now exercised special emergency powers to raid and arrest anyone suspected of being a Ghadarite. Many were caught, sometimes after ferocious gun fights. Some such as Kartar Singh Saraba were hanged, while others were given long prison sentences.

With his plans unravelling and his hideout already raided, Rashbehari had no choice but to escape to Varanasi in disguise. But he knew that he would not be safe for long in Varanasi. When Pingle was arrested in Meerut, he decided to leave the country. He purchased a first-class ticket on a passenger liner leaving Calcutta for Kobe, Japan, via Penang, Singapore and Hong Kong. The reason for an expensive first-class ticket was that Rashbehari had decided to pose as P.N. Tagore, a relative of the famous poet Rabindranath Tagore. Given the strongly hierarchical, class-conscious society of the time, Rashbehari was sure that an aristocrat from a famous family would face less scrutiny. He even managed to arrange for an identity card from the police commissioner in Calcutta!

On 12 May 1915, Rashbehari boarded the *Sanuti Maru* for Japan from Calcutta.[10] Sanyal accompanied him to the docks for a tearful farewell. Before leaving, Rashbehari gave Sanyal his Mauser pistol and a pocket watch that he had specially purchased to mark the time of his now-failed revolt. Many years later, Sanyal would pass on this watch to one of his protégés, Bhagat Singh. The watch is currently housed in a small museum collection in Hardoi.[11]

Rashbehari was leaving India for the first time and had no idea when he would come back. As it turned out, he would never see India again. He would write later in his memoirs that he spent his time on board reading the Bhagawad Gita for solace and talking to the Japanese captain.

Rashbehari was briefly questioned in Singapore and Hong Kong; his fingerprints were also taken. However, he must have put on a convincing act as none of the officials seem to have doubted the bona fides of Tagore's cousin. The

---

[10] Uma Mukherjee, *Two Great Revolutionaries*, Dey's Publishing, 1966 (reprinted in 2004).
[11] M.M. Juneja, *Biography of Bhagat Singh*, Modern Publishers, 2016.

ship reached Kobe on 5 June 1915 and a Japanese customs officer hurriedly walked up to Rashbehari and shook his hand. He told him that there were several letters waiting for him. After glancing through them, Rashbehari told officials that they were all addressed to the poet, not to P.N. Tagore. Nonetheless, he was exempted from screening and even a car was arranged to drop him off at a hotel.

The Siam Scheme and the Christmas Day Plot

The day after arriving in Kobe, Rashbehari headed to Tokyo by train. He did not know the language and worried that he would soon run out of money. With some difficulty, he hunted down Bhagwan Singh, a Ghadarite who he hoped would help him. Bhagwan Singh immediately made arrangements for his stay. He also took Rashbehari to meet the Chinese leader Sun Yat-sen, who was in exile in Japan. They would meet at Matsumotoro Café in Hibiya Park, a popular place for foreign exiles. Japan was then actively encouraging the idea of pan-Asian unity and was home to rebels of many shades. Nonetheless, intelligence reports of that time suggest that the Japanese also kept a close eye on them.

Sun Yat-sen and Rashbehari seem to have got along well. One can imagine them passionately discussing world politics at Matsumotoro Café, even as Sun's wife played the piano in the background. It was Sun Yat-sen who introduced Rashbehari to Michiru Toyama, a powerful nationalist ideologue-politician in early-twentieth-century Japan. Toyama was a strong proponent of Pan-Asianism and took the young Indian revolutionary under his wing.

Even as Rashbehari was finding his feet in Tokyo, the British decimated the Ghadarite network back in Punjab. With the arrest of Sanyal a few months later, the network in the United Provinces was also neutralized. Sanyal narrowly escaped being hanged and was sentenced to life imprisonment at the Cellular Jail.

This left Bagha Jatin's Jugantar group in Bengal as the only surviving network that could act. Importantly, it was in touch with Indian revolutionaries who had come together in Berlin with support from the German government. Known formally as the Indian Committee for National Independence—and informally as the Berlin India Committee—it included Viren Chattopadhyay (or 'Chatto'), Champak Pillai and other Indian revolutionaries who had operated in Europe in the pre-war years. Many of them had been Savarkar's followers in London and Paris. After moving from the United States to Europe, Hardayal, too, contacted the committee. The German government provided the committee with financial support and accorded it diplomatic recognition.

As it became clear that it was going to be a long-drawn-out war, the Germans began to look for ways to undermine the British Empire. An obvious ploy was to instigate armed revolt in India—the Germans were willing to supply the guns. Thus, the Berlin India Committee reached out to the Jugantar group to find out ways to smuggle a large number of arms into India. They were also in touch with Rashbehari, who was trying to procure arms in Japan and Shanghai for the same purpose.

The first German attempt to supply arms to the revolutionaries was to Ghadarites operating from Siam (now Thailand) and Burma. The idea was to foment guerrilla strikes against the colonial administration in Southeast Asia as a way to draw away British resources ahead of the main uprising in India led by Bagha Jatin. An important objective of the Siam group was to land armed guerrillas in the Andaman Islands and free the revolutionaries in the Cellular Jail.

The German consul in Shanghai arranged for a schooner, *Henry S.*, and had it loaded with arms. The ship was to pick up German military instructors arranged by the consul in Manila.[12] The schooner next headed to Thailand through the waters of the Dutch East Indies, but developed engine problems and had to dock in the Celebes, where Dutch customs authorities inspected the ship and impounded the cargo.[13] They also alerted British intelligence that something was afoot. The British chargé d'affaires in Bangkok pressured the Thai authorities to arrest key Ghadarites. A German agent, Vincent Kraft, was similarly arrested in Singapore and blurted out the plan. The whole scheme, therefore, ended in failure. Nonetheless, a small but dedicated group of Ghadarites continued to operate from Thailand for the next few decades and played an important role in the Second World War.

Tiger Jatin

Jyotindra Nath Mukherjee was born in December 1880 in Nadia district of Bengal. He belonged to an educated and socially well-connected family. As a young man, he was a naturally gifted sportsman and a daredevil. In 1906, he and his friends were walking through the jungle near his village, when they were attacked by a royal Bengal tiger. Jatin wrestled the tiger with his bare hands and even managed

---

[12] Harish K. Puri, *Ghadar Movement: A Short History,* National Book Trust, 2011.
[13] Peter Hopkirk, *On Secret Service East of Constantinople: The Plot to Bring Down the British Empire,* John Murray, 1994.

to kill it with a small knife he was carrying. Although badly injured, he survived and earned himself the nickname Bagha Jatin (Tiger Jatin).

Bagha Jatin came in contact with Aurobindo Ghosh in 1903 and soon became part of the Anushilan Samiti network. As he was frequently in Darjeeling for his job as a government clerk, he was given the role of organizing units in north Bengal. After the original Anushilan Samiti became leaderless following the Alipore Bomb Case, the movement broke up into many small units, which often worked at cross purposes. Bagha Jatin painstakingly brought together a core team—the Jugantar group—and built a working relationship with some of the better Anushilan Samiti units, such as the ones in Dacca, Barishal and Chandernagore. He also orchestrated a number of targeted killings of police officers and their collaborators. The authorities suspected him of links with the revolutionaries, sacked him from his government job and arrested him, but they did not initially work out that he was the mastermind.

The meeting in Dakshineshwar with Rashbehari in 1913 drew Bagha Jatin into the Ghadarite plan of triggering a wider rebellion in the country. However, after the police raids and arrests in Punjab and the United Provinces, his was the only cohesive group left standing by mid-1915. The Germans were in touch with the Jugantar leadership through the Berlin India Committee. The failure of the Siam scheme had been a setback, but the Germans decided that they would still go ahead with the plan to land a large number of arms on the east coast of India. The Jugantar network began to secretly drill and train youth across Bengal, in many cases using the traditional akhadas. One of the local organizers in the Nadia-

Murshidabad belt was sixteen-year-old Nalinaksha Sanyal. His elder brother, Anadi Kanta, had long been part of the Anushilan Samiti.

The plan was to land a large consignment of arms from New York on the coast of Bengal and Orissa (now Odisha) in August-September 1915. Elaborate arrangements were made to distribute and disperse the guns to the units across Bengal. These armed guerrillas were to converge on Calcutta on Christmas Day, when senior British officials traditionally attended a lunch and a ball hosted by the viceroy. Bagha Jatin scouted the coast and decided on two landing spots—one near Balasore on the Orissa coast and one in Raimangal, a rivulet in the Sunderbans in Bengal. Feelers were sent out to engage with the Rajput troops then stationed at Fort William, Calcutta. Dynamite was procured for blowing up railway bridges to delay the arrival of relief troops.

Unfortunately, due to a coordination error, the ship carrying the consignment of arms from New York never arrived, and the whole elaborate plan fell apart. Bagha Jatin waited in a small hideout near Balasore for the arms. Unknown to him, not only was the consignment lost, but British intelligence also had a sound sense of the contours of the plan by the beginning of September 1915. Charles Tegart, widely regarded as the best anti-insurgency intelligence officer in the empire, took over the case in Calcutta. Multiple police raids were carried out in Bengal and a lead brought them to Odisha.

On the evening of 6 September, Bagha Jatin received information from a local supporter that a large police contingent had arrived in the vicinity. He immediately realized that they were looking for him. He and his four companions picked up their Mausers and ammunition, and hid in the surrounding countryside. Unfortunately, the villagers mistook them for dacoits and informed the police. Very soon the police contingent arrived, and the fugitives were forced to flee. They crossed a rivulet and took up positions on a mound. A fierce gunfight followed, until two of the revolutionaries were killed and Bagha Jatin was fatally wounded. With ammunition running low, the remaining two surrendered. Bagha Jatin was taken to a nearby hospital but passed away the following day.[14]

This was followed by a series of raids across Bengal over the next three months. Hundreds of suspected revolutionaries were searched and arrested. Nalinaksha Sanyal's home in the village of Dhoradaha was also raided, but he managed to destroy all evidence before the police arrived. After being interrogated for several days, he was let off for lack of incriminating evidence.

An important reason that the German arms shipments to India repeatedly failed was that British intelligence knew what the Germans were attempting, thanks to the capture of German agent Vincent Kraft in Singapore. Maps of Bengal were found on him, in which certain points were marked along the coast. Kraft agreed to fully cooperate with the British in exchange for a substantial sum of money and permission to emigrate to the United States under a new name.[15]

An equally important source of information was a Czech nationalist and agent named Emmanuel Viktor Voska, who was operating in the United States. At this time, the Czechs were trying to free themselves from the Austrians. The Ghadarite coordinator in New York was Chandra Kanta Chakravarty. He had a Czech housekeeper, who reported back to Voska about

---

[14] Uma Mukherjee, *Two Great Revolutionaries*, Dey's Publishing, 1966 (reprinted in 2004).
[15] Peter Hopkirk, *On Secret Service East of Constantinople: The Plot to Bring Down the British Empire*, John Murray, 1994.

everything he saw and heard, especially about Chandra Kanta's dealings with German diplomats. Voska, in turn, reported this to British intelligence. Thus, the British were able to triangulate the various bits of information to get a clearer picture.[16]

Within India, Charles Tegart's intelligence network was clearly hurting the revolutionaries. The latter struck back. Tegart survived several assassination attempts, but many of his colleagues were not so lucky. The biggest strike was the killing of Intelligence Branch Superintendent Basanta Chatterjee in broad daylight on the streets of Calcutta. Many people saw it but not a single witness came forward to give evidence.[17] As many as eleven intelligence officers were killed in quick succession—this was 20 per cent of the total strength of the department. The police responded with even more arrests and repression.

∽ The Hindu–German Trials ∽

The many different attempts by the revolutionaries during the First World War to end British rule in India all ended in failure. The United States entered the war on Britain's side in April 1917. The Ghadarites had been under pressure from US authorities but a formal declaration of war made things even more difficult. Dozens of Ghadarites were arrested along with their German and German-American associates for having violated American neutrality prior to the formal declaration of war.

---

[16] Prithwindra Mukherjee, *Bagha Jatin: The Revolutionary Legacy*, Indus Source Books, 2015.
[17] Richard James Popplewell, *Intelligence and Imperial Defence: British Intelligence and the Defence of the Indian Empire 1904-1924*, Routledge, 2018.

The trials in California that started in November 1917 came to be known as the Hindu-German Conspiracy trials. Among the Indians sentenced were Taraknath Das for twenty-two months, Santokh Singh for twenty-one months and Bhagwan Singh for eighteen months. These were quite mild compared to what they would have faced if handed over to the British.

The war ended in November 1918 with the defeat of the Germans. The members of the Berlin India Committee found themselves in a difficult situation as their former allies were no longer in a position to support or protect them. It was in this moment of acute uncertainty that some of them reached out to Soviet Russia. At least at first, this was not driven by any ideological affinity but by pure survival instinct, but several former nationalists would later become communists.

Despite the repeated failures to trigger a large-scale rebellion in India, the second generation of revolutionary leaders certainly ratcheted up the game. The movement had come a long way from the small number of idealists at India House and the Maniktola garden house. Their thinking was genuinely large-scale, they had links with major global powers and their support base was much wider. The British certainly took the threat seriously, judging from the resources they deployed to stamp them out. It is important, moreover, to appreciate the Ghadarite phase of the movement, to be able to understand subsequent events from the Jallianwala Bagh massacre of 1919 to the formation of the Indian National Army in 1943. Indeed, some of the consequences can be felt to this day.

Loyalists during the War

When the war was declared, many sections of the Indian elite fell over themselves to offer help to the British cause. Nowhere was this more evident than in Punjab. The old Sikh nobility was more than keen to prove the loyalty of the 'martial race'. The Chief Khalsa Diwan condemned the Ghadarites and helped recruit soldiers. Even Gandhi, newly returned to India, joined the recruitment drive despite his avowed adherence to the principals of non-violence. However, the most enthusiastic supporters of the war effort were the contractors and agents who profited handsomely from arranging supplies and recruits.

The demands became greater as the war dragged on and the death toll mounted. Recruitment quotas were set by district, or even individual village, and ever more young men were taken into the army using false promises and intimidation. In many places, the relatively wealthy purchased young men from poor families to replace their own children. In other places, they made large contributions to the Imperial War Fund. Lieutenant Governor O'Dwyer ramped up the incentives for the contractors. In addition to their monetary commission, they were given thousands of acres of irrigated farmland next to newly built canals. They were also given fancy imperial titles.

The contractors and agents quickly became a staunchly loyalist nouveau riche. In the early years, there may have been some members of the general population who voluntarily signed up for the army in exchange for regular pay or adventure. However, as the death toll mounted, voluntary recruitment all but disappeared. There are several eyewitness accounts of how local officials and agents colluded to 'herd' poor peasants into the army.

When the war was over, a 'grateful' colonial government built India Gate in New Delhi as a memorial for the tens of thousands of Indians who died fighting for someone else's empire. Many of their names are inscribed on it.

The Indian National Congress, meanwhile, had been mostly inactive in the immediate pre-war years. The split into two warring camps had significantly weakened it. It was the revolutionaries who had provided most of the political resistance during those years. Tilak returned from Mandalay Jail in mid-1914. Initially it appeared that he had mellowed in prison and even offered moral support to the war effort. However, a year later, he was back to his assertive self. Even as he tried to unite the Congress factions, he established the India Home Rule League in 1916, demanding full self-rule. The movement spread like wildfire and there was enthusiastic participation that cut across class and religion. Writings of senior British officials in 1918 show that they considered Tilak the most powerful Indian of that time.

Tilak passed away in August 1920. The momentum of the Home Rule League was used by a new leader, Mohandas Karamchand Gandhi, to build up protests against the Rowlatt Acts in 1919 and eventually the Non-Cooperation Movement in 1920–21.

♦ 5 ♦
KALA PAANI

THE ANDAMAN AND NICOBAR Islands are a string of small islands just north of Sumatra—the northern cluster is known as the Andamans and the southern as Nicobar. The name 'Andaman' derives from the Malay pronunciation of 'Hanuman'. The islands were a Danish colony in the early eighteenth century and passed into British hands by the end of the century. As early as 1789, the East India Company recognized the possibility of using one of the islands as a penal colony for convicts from the Indian mainland. However, the settlement was abandoned after just seven years because of high mortality rates among both prisoners and prison guards.

It was only after the Revolt of 1857 that the British revisited the idea of creating a penal settlement in the islands. Hundreds of rebels were sent there—many would be hanged while most others would die from diseases caused by unsanitary living conditions in an intensely hot and humid climate. Since few convicts ever returned alive, the penal colony came to be known as Kala Paani, or the 'Black Waters'. At the beginning of the twentieth century, there were 12,000 convicts scattered across the islands.

The Cellular Jail

In the nineteenth century, convicts were kept in a number of scattered settlements. However, it was decided that those deemed the most dangerous would be locked up in a single large facility in Port Blair. Completed in 1906, the huge Cellular Jail derived its name from the individual 13'6" x 7'6" cells arranged in rows along seven radials. Where the radials met, there was a central watchtower from which the guards could observe the prisoners.

The Cellular Jail soon became the preferred place to send political prisoners deemed too dangerous to execute or imprison on the mainland. This included Barin Ghosh, Ullaskar Dutt, Vinayak Savarkar, Ganesh Savarkar and others. From 1915, Ghadarite leaders such as Sachindra Nath Sanyal were also sent here. Several survivors have left vivid accounts of the horrifying conditions inside the facility.

What turned life in the Cellular Jail into a living hell was the daily regime deliberately designed to constantly humiliate and physically torment the convict. The main meal was made of 'ganji'—boiled rice stirred into a gooey porridge. It had no salt and was entirely tasteless. The prisoners were sometimes given rotis that were as tough as leather, served with watery dal and half-cooked vegetables. The food often had insects and worms, and the half-cooked vegetables were not easy to digest. Any complaint was brutally punished and resulted in

all food being withdrawn for days. So, almost all the prisoners suffered frequently from abdominal pain and diarrhoea. It was not uncommon to find a prisoner passed out in his cell in his own excrement.

The prisoners were expected to work during the day. Two kinds of tasks were commonly given. The first was coir rope-making. The prisoners had to use their bare hands to strip out the coir fibre, pound it to soften it and then braid it into rope. Each prisoner was expected to produce a minimum of three pounds of rope every day. Hard as it was, it was considered better than the task of turning the *kolhu* (oil mill). This required enormous strength and stamina, especially since this was done in the blazing tropical sun. Even a sip of water was not provided. The wardens used sticks and whips to ensure compliance. However, if they wanted to break a mentally strong prisoner, they used fetters.

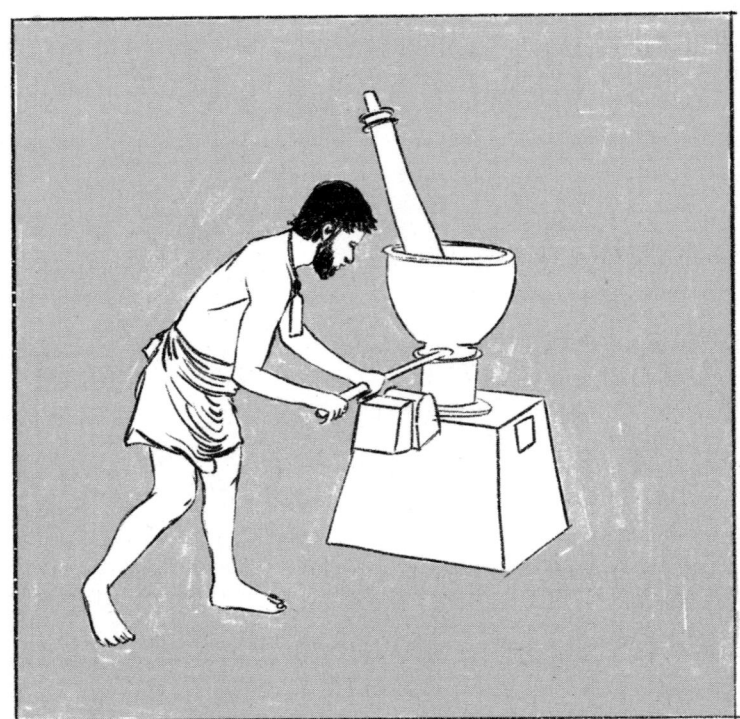

Given this inhuman treatment, it is not surprising that many prisoners contemplated suicide. In 1912, Indu Bhushan Roy hanged himself in his cell. David Barrie, who ran the facility, was furious when news of the suicide leaked out and caused a public uproar. A few weeks later, Ullaskar Dutt refused to do his assigned work of climbing into a well and lifting out buckets of water. Barrie ordered that his hands be chained and he be suspended by them from the ceiling of his cell for a week.

The pain made Ullaskar hallucinate and his screams filled the Cellular Jail. He was dragged out and found to be delirious with fever. But this did not stop his tormentors. Barrie insisted that Ullaskar was only feigning insanity to avoid work and ordered that electric shocks be administered to see if he had indeed gone insane. As the electricity passed through his body, Ullaskar screamed until he fell unconscious. He regained consciousness after three days but continued to have fits and convulsions.[1]

Vinayak Savarkar confronted Barrie about Ullaskar's condition, but he was still adamant that Ullaskar was just trying to shirk work. However, he was concerned that the incident had been witnessed by too many people and news of it would get out. He eventually allowed Ullaskar to be shifted to a mental asylum in Madras, where he would remain for twelve years.

The next act of resistance came from Nani Gopal, a seventeen-year-old revolutionary from Chinsura (now Chuchura) in Bengal. The boy refused to work the oil mill one day. He was sent away for a while to another prison on Viper Island, but when he returned, he started a hunger strike. Several other prisoners followed. Savarkar realized that this was a good time to extract some concessions. In return for

[1] Vikram Sampath, *Savarkar: Echoes from a Forgotten Past 1883-1924*, Penguin India, 2019.

convincing the prisoners to end their strike, Savarkar was able to negotiate small improvements in their lives—some time for social interaction between prisoners, access to books and papers and a supply of slates, paper and pencils for teaching the less educated.[2] After this incident, Savarkar became the de facto leader of the convicted revolutionaries.

Jallianwala Bagh

The First World War ended in November 1918, and the Indian regiments began to come home. The colonial administration was nervous as the soldiers had been radicalized with Ghadarite ideas before they had been deployed and had come within an inch of revolt in 1915. As experienced war veterans, they were now even more dangerous. Not only were they conversant with the latest military technology but had also stood shoulder-to-shoulder with European troops in the trenches. Therefore, they were not in awe of the white man. Nowhere was the nervousness greater than in Punjab.

The British authorities decided to give themselves ever more draconian powers. The Anarchical and Revolutionary Crimes Act (popularly known as the Rowlatt Acts) was introduced, consisting of two bills specifically designed to target revolutionaries. They allowed for speedy trials by a special court that could meet in-camera and take consideration of evidence not allowed under the Indian Evidence Act, and there was no appeal. The provincial government was given the power to search without a warrant and to confine any suspect without explanation. In other words, it effectively removed all legal protection for the Indian population.

[2] *Ibid.*

The first of the two bills was passed on 18 March 1919 and enacted before it was even published, despite the fact that only one Indian member voted in its favour. There was an immediate backlash. Three Indians resigned from the Imperial Legislative Council—Madan Mohan Malaviya, Mazharul Haque and Mohammad Ali Jinnah.[3] The political movement against the laws gathered pace under the leadership of Gandhi. This was the first time that his approach of passive resistance *(satyagraha)* was deployed on a national level.

Gandhi announced a general strike on 30 March and then again on 6 April. The strikes were successful, with shops and other establishments being closed, and protesters gathering in large numbers. However, they were not entirely peaceful and there were clashes in Delhi and Ahmedabad. Several people were killed in police firing. Gandhi went to Punjab but was forcibly made to deboard the train near Delhi and sent to Bombay under escort before being freed.

Meanwhile, in Punjab, Lieutenant Governor Michael O'Dwyer was determined to quash any protests with an iron hand. Two local businessmen in Amritsar, Mahasha Rattan Chand and Chaudhuri Bugga Mall, had been setting up wrestling akhadas in and around the city. The authorities became suspicious when the two organized a large Ram Navami celebration on 9 April, which attracted significant Muslim participation. A display of Hindu–Muslim unity was something that the authorities saw as a threat. Chand and Mall also invited two well-known INC leaders, Dr Satyapal and Dr Saifuddin Kitchlew, to speak on the Rowlatt Acts.

At 7 p.m. on 9 April, the local administration in Amritsar received orders from O'Dwyer's office to arrest Satyapal and Kitchlew. By the next morning, news of the arrest spread

---
[3] Kishwar Desai, *Jallianwala Bagh, 1919: The Real Story*, Westland Books, 2018.

across Amritsar and protesters began to gather at Hall Bazaar. Around 11.30 a.m., a group of protesters decided to walk to the office of the deputy commissioner to petition for their release. The group was unarmed and the protests were entirely peaceful. As they made their way over a railway overbridge, they were stopped by a military picket. An argument broke out, and at some point, two British soldiers lost their patience and fired into the crowd, killing four protesters and wounding several more.

The crowd fled back to the city and reassembled at Hall Bazaar. The sight of the dead and wounded had agitated the mood greatly, but the crowd was still peaceful. More people began to assemble, perhaps as many as 30,000. Some of the protesters decided to go back to the railway overbridge—some may even have thrown stones at the picket. Suddenly the soldiers let loose a volley of gunfire that killed another twenty people and left many more badly wounded.

News of the second massacre reached the main gathering at Hall Bazaar. As some of the bodies were brought back, the crowd grew angrier. Some people attacked British-linked institutions in the vicinity—National Bank, Chartered Bank, Alliance Bank and the Church Missionary Society's Girls Normal School. Three European bank managers were killed. A female missionary was beaten, even as another British woman, a doctor, narrowly escaped. In all, five British civilians were killed by the mob.

The press reports of the time presented the mob attack as unprovoked. The names and personal details of all the European casualties were widely reported, but we have almost no information about the Indians killed.

By 11 April, more military contingents arrived in Amritsar. Rattan Chand and Bugga Mall were arrested and sent to the

Cellular Jail. Gholam Jilani, a local imam who had helped garner Muslim participation in the Ram Navami festivities, was picked up by the police and subjected to extreme torture. Another 200 locals were arrested and tried under martial law for the attacks on the Europeans.

On the night of 11 April, Brigadier-General Reginald Dyer arrived from Jullundur to take charge of the city. Military pickets were set up all over the city. Before dawn on 12 April, Dyer had cut off water and electricity supplies to the city. A group of local activists called a public meeting in Jallianwala Bagh on the afternoon of 13 April to discuss the situation. It was a Sunday as well as Baisakhi—a holy day for Hindus and Sikhs. Many people from the surrounding villages had come to visit the Golden Temple. Despite heavy military presence, the morning appeared peaceful, except that very few shops were open due to the strike.

Jallianwala Bagh is located in the old, crowded part of Amritsar, barely a stone's throw from the Golden Temple. It is a sizeable open area where local children played, people gathered for festivals and occasionally public meetings were held. Importantly, it only had one narrow entrance-exit. Around 4 p.m. on 13 April, there were 8,000–10,000 people in the park. Perhaps 2,000 or so were there to attend the public meeting, but the majority were casual visitors.

The first sign of trouble was a plane flying in circles above the city. Ground reports and the aerial survey gave Dyer a fairly good idea of the number of people in the park. He placed pickets on the roads leading to the park, with orders to shoot anyone escaping from it. Then, he arrived at the entrance of the Jallianwala Bagh with a contingent of troops armed with .303 Lee-Enfield rifles and two armoured cars with machine guns. The cars were left outside to guard the entrance. He then marched the troops into the park and lined them up next to the only exit route.

Without any warning, Dyer ordered the soldiers to fire at the unarmed civilians. They fired 1,650 rounds, or 33 per person.[4] There was mayhem as people began to drop dead. Several more died in the stampede that followed, while

[4] Kishwar Desai, *Jallianwalla Bagh 1919: The Real Story*, Westland Books, 2018.

many fell into an open well even as others tried to escape by climbing the walls. Many more were shot at the pickets as they tried to make their way out.

The official death toll was initially put at just 250 and later raised to 379, but most reliable estimates put it at around 1,000.[5] Dyer said at the subsequent inquiry that his act was deliberate and that he had been prevented from killing even more because the narrow passage did not allow the entry of the armoured cars. All eyewitness accounts confirm that the casualties included a large number of children.

The events in Amritsar were not isolated. There was a broader attempt to batter the population of Punjab into submission. Lieutenant Governor O'Dwyer, for instance, ordered the use of military aircraft to bomb the civilian population. Thus, a day after the massacre in Amritsar, an aircraft flew low over Gujranwala, dropping bombs and firing on any large group of Indians that he could see from the air. Arbitrary racist punishments were also imposed in several towns.

Jallianwala Bagh still exists in Amritsar and is today a national monument. One can walk through the narrow entrance used by Dyer. The walls still bear the bullet holes.

The Aftermath

The British initially tried to suppress news of the atrocities being perpetrated in Punjab, but the scale of events was too large to remain hidden for long. It led to a wave of horror and revulsion across the country. The poet Rabindranath Tagore returned his knighthood in protest, with the words:

---

[5] *Struggle for Freedom*, edited by R.C. Majumdar, Bharatiya Vidya Bhavan, 1969 (reprinted in 1978). This is part of *The History and Culture of the Indian People series*, Volume XI.

> 'The very least I can do for my country is to take all consequences upon myself in giving voice to the protest of the millions of my countrymen, surprised into a dumb anguish of terror.'

The Congress instituted a committee of inquiry that collected eyewitness accounts of what had happened.

The colonial government, however, continued to support Dyer, and even gave him a promotion—albeit later reversed. They eventually pronounced a mild censure on him and removed him from active service, while O'Dwyer was absolved of all responsibility. The British press and prominent individuals such as Rudyard Kipling were almost entirely in Dyer's camp. A fund was opened by *The Morning Post* in London to collect money for him—it was supported by most English-language newspapers in India. The resident European community in India came out in full support of Dyer. English ladies in Mussoorie set up a Dyer Appreciation Fund and collected a large sum that they presented to the man.[6] The dominant British view was that Dyer had saved the empire from another 1857.

What was worse was the attitude of the loyalist Punjabi elite. Both the traditional elite and the newly rich contractor class were effusive in their support of O'Dwyer and Dyer. They organized farewell dinners for them and raised money for generous gifts. Just a few weeks after the massacre, the head of the Akal Takht, Arur Singh, invited Dyer to the Golden Temple and presented him with a *siropa* (robe of honour).[7]

---

[6] *Struggle for Freedom*, edited by R.C. Majumdar, Bharatiya Vidya Bhavan, 1969 (reprinted in 1978). This is part of *The History and Culture of the Indian People* series, Volume XI.
[7] Kishwar Desai, *Jallianwalla Bagh 1919*, Westland, 2018. Also Divya Goyal, 'Judging the Erstwhile Royals: An Unkind Cut or a Bitter Truth?', *The Indian Express*, 13 April 2019, https://indianexpress.com/article/india/jallianwala-bagh-judging-the-erstwhile-royals-an-unkind-cut-or-a-bitter-truth5673646/

Return from Hell

By the end of 1919, it was obvious even to the most optimistic colonial official that the Jallianwala Bagh massacre had been a strategic mistake, as it had inflamed Indian nationalism. The government began to look for ways to soften the mood. One of the measures was to release some of the revolutionary leaders incarcerated in various jails. Among those released from the Cellular Jail were Barin Ghosh and Sachindra Nath Sanyal.

In his book *Bandi Jeevan,* Sanyal describes the initial exhilaration and then the somewhat mixed feelings at the realization that most of his fellow convicts would remain in prison. He felt almost guilty leaving them behind. It was another twenty days before the ship arrived and he remained in his cell until he boarded the ship to Calcutta along with Barin and the others.

On reaching Calcutta, they were all taken to the police headquarters. They sat around for hours for some paperwork to get done. At some point, Sanyal lost his patience and just walked out. No one stopped him. He did not have any money and did not have the exact address of his cousin who lived in Calcutta. He asked a young man for help with directions and made friends with him. Sanyal writes that he tried to ascertain his new friend's political views and to recruit him for the revolutionary cause. He had been free for only a couple of hours and was already back to recruiting. He did not succeed, but he did manage to find his cousin's house and enjoyed his first home-cooked meal in years!

A couple of days later, Sanyal took a train to Varanasi. His main concern was to find a way to free the remaining political prisoners from the Cellular Jail, in particular Bhai Parmanand and Vinayak Savarkar. With this in mind, he met Madan Mohan Malaviya, who was then building Banaras Hindu University. Malaviya gave him a patient hearing but did not offer any concrete assistance.

Disappointed, Sanyal reached out to every INC leader who was willing to meet him. He recounts how he met Jawaharlal Nehru in Gorakhpur. After hearing him out, Nehru commented, *'At a time that we are planning to go to jail, you want us to help others come out of prison?'*[8] This comment stunned Sanyal. He realized that most INC leaders simply did not appreciate the difference between conditions in a normal prison and those in the Cellular Jail. Sanyal kept up his efforts and attended an INC special session in Calcutta. Lala Lajpat Rai, who was presiding over the session, met Sanyal and immediately offered his unconditional backing. Others such as Bipin Pal and Chittaranjan Das also offered help. They arranged for a speaking slot at the Nagpur Congress in December 1920.

The Nagpur Congress is today remembered for the adoption of Gandhi's proposal for a nationwide Non-Cooperation Movement. Less remembered is the fact that Sanyal spoke at the event about the treatment of political prisoners in the Cellular Jail. Narayan Savarkar, Vinayak's younger brother, was also present on the stage. A resolution was passed, asking for better treatment and release of the imprisoned revolutionaries. As a result, a few more revolutionaries were released but Vinayak Savarkar was brought back to the mainland only in May 1921 and held in Ratnagiri Jail for another three years. Thereafter, he would be restricted to Ratnagiri district under strict conditions for thirteen more years.

---

[8] Sachindra Nath Sanyal, *Bandi Jeevan*, reprinted in Hindi by Sakshi Prakashan, 2015.

Khilafat and Non-Cooperation

The post-war terms offered by the Allies effectively called for the dismemberment of the Ottoman Empire. As the Ottoman Sultan was considered by many Sunnis to be the Caliph, this led to discontent among pan-Islamists in India. Gandhi saw this as an opportunity to increase the Muslim community's participation in the freedom struggle. The result was the Khilafat Movement, launched in August 1920. It was a controversial decision, since it made Muslim participation in a national freedom movement contingent on external loyalties. For the moment, however, there were loud proclamations of Hindu-Muslim unity and a palpable increase in Muslim involvement.

Gandhi now sought to use the momentum to launch the Non-Cooperation Movement, where Indians would progressively boycott all institutions related to the colonial administration—courts, offices, educational institutions, legislatures, titles/awards and so on. At the same time, Indians would adopt 'swadeshi', meaning they would boycott all foreign-made goods. This was conceptually similar to what had been done in 1905–06, except that Gandhi additionally insisted on traditional modes of production, such as hand-spinning and weaving. This was a break from the original emphasis on modernization.

Many senior leaders in the INC were sceptical of Gandhi's new methods. Madan Mohan Malaviya, Annie Besant, M.A. Jinnah and Chittaranjan Das initially opposed the proposals. However, Gandhi was able to carry the resolution at the Nagpur Congress with 1,886 votes against 884. With Tilak having passed away in August, this marked the emergence of Gandhi as the pre-eminent leader of the INC.

Into 1921, it became apparent that Gandhi's new approach was attracting widespread public participation. Many revolutionaries, even those who may have been initially dismissive of the idea of passive resistance, joined the movement. Nevertheless, several key revolutionary leaders stayed away. Sanyal remained sceptical about the ability of the movement to extract real concessions. He preferred to use this time to expand links with trade unions and peasant movements. Sri Aurobindo had withdrawn from political activity, but there were still many supporters who hoped that he would return, especially after Tilak's death. Even Gandhi sent his son, Devdas, to Pondicherry (now Puducherry) to elicit his support, but was refused. Sri Aurobindo was unconvinced by Gandhian methods. He would mock the extreme adherence to non-violence as 'getting beaten with joy'. When the Non-Cooperation Movement was launched, he predicted that it would end 'in great confusion or in a great fiasco'.[9]

Just as the Non-Cooperation Movement reached its climax in the second half of 1921, its internal contradictions also came to the fore. The Khilafat Movement had mobilized the Muslims along communal rather than nationalist lines, and this led to widespread riots and violence. C. Gopalan Nair, a retired civil servant, witnessed the riots and published an account just two years later.[10]

Gandhi's response to these incidents was disappointing. He initially denied the violence and then tried to downplay its links to the Khilafat Movement. Despite this, the Non-Cooperation Movement was still going strong in January 1922. On 5 February, a police officer had an altercation with some volunteers manning a picket in front of a liquor shop

[9] Peter Heehs, *The Lives of Sri Aurobindo*, Columbia University Press, 2008.
[10] C. Gopalan Nair, *The Moplah Rebellion: 1921*, Norman Printing Bureau, 1923.

in the village bazaar of Chauri Chaura, near Gorakhpur. The police beat up some volunteers and in response several hundred villagers gathered at the police station to lodge a protest. Some local elders calmed the situation down and the crowd began to disperse. Suddenly, the police decided to fire on some of the stragglers. At least two villagers were killed. This incensed the crowd, which now returned in full fury. The policeman bolted themselves inside the station but the mob set it on fire. About twenty-two trapped policemen died.

When Gandhi heard about the incident, he unilaterally decided to withdraw the Non-Cooperation Movement. Many Congress leaders felt that a single incident should not derail a national movement, but Gandhi was adamant. The British took advantage of the confusion to make arrests and break down all opposition.

Chittaranjan's Recruits

The sudden withdrawal of the Non-Cooperation Movement and the subsequent arrests left the INC in disarray. Chittaranjan Das, a successful lawyer, became the effective leader of those opposed to Gandhi. Even moderates such as Motilal Nehru and Vithalbhai Patel joined him. They formed a group within the Congress known as the Swaraj Party, which was willing to participate in the provincial councils being set up by the colonial administration.

An important source of Das's growing political heft was the systematic absorption into the Congress of former revolutionaries or those with revolutionary sympathies. As a young lawyer, Das had defended Aurobindo Ghosh during the Alipore trials of 1908–09 and, therefore, had a long relationship with the revolutionary movement. In the early 1920s, Das brought in two young men into the Congress who would play an important role in subsequent events—Subhas Chandra Bose and Nalinaksha Sanyal.

Subhas was born on 23 January 1897 in Cuttack to a lawyer, Janakinath Bose, and his wife, Prabhavati. Theirs was an upper-middle-class Bengali family originally from Calcutta. When he was around fifteen, Subhas moved to Calcutta. This is also the time when he discovered the ideas and writings of Swami Vivekananda. This would have a profound impact on him, so much so that for a while he contemplated becoming a monk.

During the summer vacation of 1914, Subhas travelled with a friend to various pilgrimage sites—Rishikesh, Haridwar, Mathura and Varanasi. He returned to Calcutta, having decided against becoming a monk, but would retain a strongly religious streak throughout his life.

After high school, Subhas joined Presidency College in Calcutta, where in 1916 he participated in an explicitly political activity. Edward Oaten, a history professor said to hold racist views, got into an altercation with a group of students. Led by Subhas, the students demanded an apology and went on strike. Oaten and the principal met student representatives and settled the matter. However, the very next day, Oaten turned out ten of the twelve students from his class for having participated in the strike. He also manhandled a student. This enraged the students, and a group of them gave Oaten a beating. It is unclear if Subhas hit the professor, but he was certainly present. In any case, as the leader of the strike, he was blamed for the incident and expelled from the college.[11]

Subhas spent a year back in Cuttack before he enrolled in Scottish Church College to read philosophy. He got first-

---

[11] Sugata Bose, *His Majesty's Opponent*, Penguin India, 2011.

class marks and was placed second in Calcutta University's order of merit. For his master's degree, he wanted to study experimental psychology, but his father persuaded him to go to England and attempt the ICS examinations. Thus, in September 1919, Subhas sailed to England and, like Aurobindo Ghosh, enrolled in Cambridge while he prepared for the examination. When the results of the 1920 examination were published, he was surprised to find that he had stood fourth. Subhas faced the same dilemma that Aurobindo Ghosh had a generation earlier—should he serve a colonial government that suppressed his people? To the great disappointment of his family, Subhas decided to opt out.

Subhas sailed back to India in July 1921. By coincidence, Rabindranath Tagore was on the same ship and they spent a lot of time discussing the evolving political situation. Tagore was not in favour of the Non-Cooperation Movement, as he felt that it would permanently damage and politicize institutions such as universities. He also felt that the movement was unnecessarily burdened by Gandhi's personal aversion to modern technology. The idealistic young man was not entirely convinced by Tagore's arguments. So, when he landed in Bombay, he immediately made his way to Mani Bhawan to meet Gandhi but was disappointed with the meeting. Bose recalled the meeting in his book *The Indian Struggle*:

> *But though I tried to persuade myself at that time that there must be a lack of understanding on my part, my reason told me clearly, again and again, that there was a deplorable lack of clarity in the plan which the Mahatma had formulated and that he himself did not have a clear idea of the successive stages of the campaign which would bring India to her cherished goal of freedom.*[12]

[12] Subhas Chandra Bose, *The Indian Struggle (1920-1934)*, Abhishek Publications (reprinted in 2019).

Disappointed, Subhas returned to Calcutta. A few days later, he met Chittaranjan Das, with whom he had been corresponding from Cambridge. Subhas immediately felt that 'here was a man who knew what he was about'. He would later write, 'I felt I had found a Leader and I meant to follow him.' [13]

Das was initially not in favour of the Non-Cooperation Movement but took to it enthusiastically once a majority of the INC members supported it. Subhas became his chief organizer for strikes in Calcutta. In December 1921, both Subhas and Das were arrested. This was the first time that Subhas had been sent to prison.

When Gandhi withdrew the movement, the British were jubilant. Prime Minister David Lloyd George made a speech in August 1922, where he congratulated the ICS for suppressing the freedom movement and being a staunchly loyal 'steel frame'.[14] This phrase is attributed today to Vallabhbhai Patel, but was originally used by Lloyd George to describe how firmly the colonial administration had stood up through the world war, the Ghadar Movement, the Jallianwala Bagh massacre and finally the Non-Cooperation Movement.

When Subhas was released from jail in September, there was news of devastating floods in north Bengal. He immediately headed there, along with Nalinaksha Sanyal, to organize relief efforts. The relief work was widely appreciated and helped Subhas build a core team, but it did not change the fact that the wider movement was in shambles.

The Swaraj Party now decided to break away from Gandhi's approach and contest elections, including those to the Calcutta Corporation. They won a comfortable majority in the municipal elections of 1924. Thus, Das became the mayor of Calcutta, Hussain Shaheed Suhrawardy became the deputy

[13] *Ibid*
[14] *Ibid.*

mayor and twenty-seven-year-old Subhas became the chief executive officer of the administration. Subhas threw himself into administrative work, and it appears he rather enjoyed it. Unfortunately, this did not last long as the intelligence agencies were convinced that he was secretly building an underground revolutionary network.

On 25 October 1924, the police arrested Subhas under the Regulation III of 1818. Under this provision, the colonial administration could detain anyone indefinitely without a trial or even making charges against them public. He was briefly held in Berhampore and then shifted to Mandalay. The untimely death of Das in June 1925 came as a blow. Subhas had lost his mentor and he would now have to evolve quickly into a leader in his own right.

In October 1925, the prisoners, led by Subhas, requested the Mandalay Jail authorities for permission to celebrate Durga Puja. Permission was initially granted but abruptly

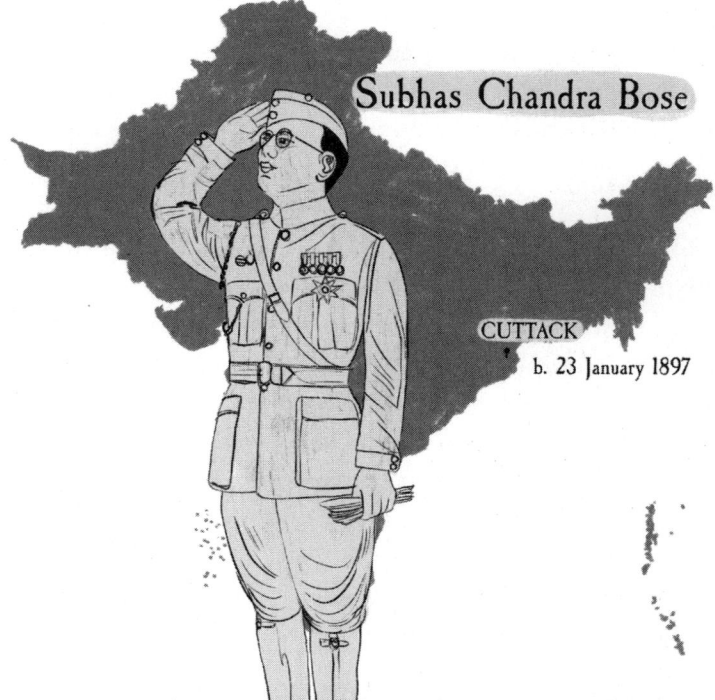

Subhas Chandra Bose

CUTTACK
b. 23 January 1897

reversed by the government—the jail superintendent was censured for granting approval. The Hindu prisoners were particularly incensed when the Christian convicts were allowed to celebrate Christmas a few months later. In response, Subhas led a fifteen-day hunger strike in February 1926. Despite government efforts to keep it quiet, news of the hunger strike was reported in the Swarajist newspaper *Forward* and caused an uproar. The government was eventually forced to back down and the hunger strike was withdrawn. Unfortunately, Subhas's health kept deteriorating. The steady loss of weight led to concerns that he might have contracted tuberculosis, considered a deadly disease at that time.

The Bose family lobbied to have Subhas released. The government offered to release him on condition that he would go directly to Europe for treatment and not return to India until 1930. The offer was rejected. The government then decided to shift him to Almora Jail in the Himalayas, where the weather was considered healthy for tuberculosis patients. He was brought back to Calcutta in May 1927, and the new governor Sir Stanley Jackson ordered his release. Thus, after two and a half years of detention without trial, Subhas was free.

The Rebel Scholar

Nalinaksha Sanyal was born in November 1898 in the village of Dhoradaha in the Nadia district of Bengal. His family was educated but not well off; they owned a patch of land and partly depended on agricultural income. Nalinaksha's elder brother, Anadi Kanta, was a member of the Anushilan Samiti.

During 1914–15, Nalinaksha was an active member of Bagha Jatin's Jugantar network and was involved in building a revolutionary network in the Nadia–Murshidabad belt. He was arrested during the police crackdown following Bagha Jatin's death, but was eventually let off on lack of incriminating evidence. He remained part of the surviving group of Jugantar revolutionaries led by Amarendra Nath Chatterjee in Nadia and worked closely with the Anushilan Samiti network run by Pratul Chandra Ganguli in nearby Murshidabad.

Not surprisingly, he was constantly on the police radar. In 1916, he was arrested at 4 a.m. on the last day of his intermediate of arts examinations. Just hours earlier, Nalinaksha had seen a suspicious person loitering around his home and guessed that he might be an informer. Therefore, he had burnt all the papers and hidden his pistol. The authorities, nonetheless, were not going to let him off so easily and hauled him before the magistrate. After much begging, the magistrate let him appear for the paper under police surveillance and he was taken to the lock-up immediately afterwards. Despite this, Sanyal would be placed eleventh in the overall order of merit in Calcutta University.[15]

Nalinaksha joined Presidency College and immediately became the leader of a group of students sympathetic to the revolutionary cause. He and his brother were soon arrested under the Defence of India Act for 'terrorist' activities after a number of intelligence officers were killed in Calcutta. Again, he was let off after weeks of severe interrogation for lack of evidence, even though the police were certain he had links with armed groups. His brother Anadi was not so lucky and died of internal injuries caused by torture in Rangpur Jail. This incident had a big influence on Nalinaksha.

On his release, Chittaranjan Das reached out to Nalinaksha and brought him into the fold of the Congress.

---

[15] Birth Centenary Brochure of Dr. Nalinaksha Sanyal, published 1998.

In 1920, he attended the INC session in Nagpur. The session included the first All India Students Conference, where Nalinaksha led the student delegation from Bengal. It was at this event that Nalinaksha met many national-level leaders, including Sachindra Nath Sanyal. The Nagpur session endorsed Gandhi's Non-Cooperation Movement, but, like many activists with a revolutionary bent, Nalinaksha remained sceptical. Nevertheless, he loyally participated in the movement after Das endorsed it.

In 1921, Nalinaksha joined the MA course in economics at Calcutta University. By this time, he was the leader of a large network of student activists. Their work was not always related to the freedom movement. For instance, Bengal was then in the grip of a cholera epidemic and thousands were dying from it. The very poor, particularly Dalits, had no medical help. The fear of infection was so great that there were many instances when no one was willing to perform the last rites when a person died. Nalinaksha organized a group of students who provided help to patients without support, and performed the last rites too. In fact, he learnt Hindu funeral rituals and performed the last rites of scores himself.

After finishing his MA, Nalinaksha took up the job of a lecturer at Krishnath College in Berhampore. He was also the key coordinator of the Swarajist faction of the INC in the Nadia-Murshidabad belt. The college became a hotbed of revolutionary activity during this period. It was during this time that the nationalist poet Kazi Nazrul Islam was held in Berhampore Jail. The poet and the activist became the best of friends, a relationship they would maintain for the rest of their lives.

Das's death in 1925 was a blow to Nalinaksha. He, too, had lost his mentor. A year later, he was able to secure a scholarship from a wealthy patron, Raja Manindra Chandra Nundy of Kasimbazar, who funded his PhD at the London School of Economics.

Rashbehari's Bride

Rashbehari Bose had arrived in Japan as Rabindranath Tagore's cousin but his efforts to procure arms for Bagha Jatin did not escape the attention of British intelligence. All pretence was dropped after Rashbehari organized a public event for Lala Lajpat Rai in Tokyo on 17 November 1915. Japan was nominally a British ally at that time and came under intense diplomatic pressure to deport Rashbehari along with Heramba Lal Gupta, the representative of the Berlin India Committee in Tokyo. The Japanese government eventually issued orders on 28 November, stating that the two had to leave the country by 2 December.

The Japanese press was outraged as this was seen as an insult to the country's sovereignty and the betrayal of a fellow Asian. Nonetheless, on 1 December, the Chief of Metropolitan Police issued a statement that the two would be handed over to the British if they did not leave the country by the next morning. Desperate, Rashbehari reached out to his friend Toyama, who invited them home for a farewell party that evening.

Heramba Lal and Rashbehari arrived at Toyama's house in the evening. They were tailed by a couple of policemen. As is customary, they took off their shoes and went inside while the policemen waited outside. Once inside, the Indians were herded barefoot through a kitchen back door that led into a neighbour's house. After exiting into a different street, they walked to a getaway car waiting for them. The policemen, meanwhile, were still in front of Toyama's house.[16]

Rashbehari and Heramba Lal were then taken to a small stand-alone studio at the back of Nakamuraya bakery, where they were to stay in hiding. The bakery owner, Koko, knew some English and translated the numerous news reports that appeared over the next few days about their disappearance. It was clear that public opinion was strongly in their favour.

After two months, Heramba Lal had had enough. He escaped one evening through a window and moved to the home of a Japanese friend. Rashbehari was now all alone in the studio. He decided to learn Japanese and taught himself the basics using a bilingual textbook.

Life settled into a pattern until an almost-forgotten incident changed the situation. A British naval vessel fired on a Japanese ship, *Tenyo-Maru*, and forced it to dock in Hong Kong. Seven Indians were taken off and sent to Singapore, effectively kidnapped. The Japanese lodged a strong protest and retaliated by withdrawing the deportation orders against Rashbehari and Heramba Lal. They were now free. Toyama even arranged for a suitable house for Rashbehari.[17]

A few weeks after moving into his new home, Rashbehari organized a dinner to thank everyone who had helped him. Everyone was surprised when he gave a speech in Japanese. They were also treated to an Indian meal prepared by Rashbehari himself.

Rashbehari now became an important member of the Pan-Asian movement, which was quite strong in Japan. Despite his changed status, however, he knew that agents hired by British intelligence were keeping an eye on him and tailing his Japanese friends. He changed homes several

---

[16] Takeshi Nakajima, *Bose of Nakamuraya: An Indian Revolutionary in Japan*, translated from Japanese by Prem Motwani, Promilla & Co, 2005.
[17] Ibid.

times, but the agents always found him. There was constant fear that they would harm him or that the British would find an opportunity to arm-twist the Japanese government into handing him over. Tomaya suggested that Rashbehari marry the bakery owners' daughter, Toshiko, and become a Japanese citizen. Rashbehari and Toshiko had fallen in love when he was hiding in the studio.

They got married in a private ceremony at Toyama's house on 9 July 1918. They had two children, and Rashbehari became a naturalized Japanese citizen in 1923. Unfortunately,

Toshiko came down with a severe case of pneumonia in 1924 and passed away. Rashbehari later wrote, 'Our married life was very short but it was bliss. I had a feeling that I enjoyed total happiness during those years.' [18]

A part of the Nakamuraya bakery was later converted into a café that served Indian curries. This was Rashbehari's contribution and it was a big success. Many of Tokyo's elite and intelligentsia came there frequently to eat authentic curry. Rashbehari was probably not the first to introduce Indian cuisine to Japan, but he was certainly the one who popularized it. He soon became known widely as 'Bose of Nakamuraya'. Japanese writers of the inter-war period often mention the café.

---

[18] *Ibid.*

◆ 6 ◆
THE HINDUSTAN REPUBLICAN ASSOCIATION

WHILE THE NON-COOPERATION Movement was gathering momentum in 1921, many revolutionaries were influenced by Chittaranjan Das's decision to support Gandhi. Sachindra Nath Sanyal appreciated that Gandhi's softer approach made it easier for more people to join the national movement but decided to stay away himself. Instead, he briefly tried his hand at different things, including managing a brick kiln. Eventually, at the request of Das's brother-in-law, he took charge of the labour union in Jamshedpur.

The Jamshedpur union was in shambles when he arrived, but within a few months, its membership rose and the finances improved. Sanyal also got married to a spirited young lady, Pratibha. Nevertheless, he still yearned to re-ignite the revolutionary movement. In early 1922, he moved back to the United Provinces and began to re-establish contact with various groups. This time he established a base in Allahabad (now Prayagraj), although he also had operations in Varanasi.[1]

The collapse of the Non-Cooperation Movement after the Chauri Chaura incident dramatically changed the political landscape. Many revolutionaries were disillusioned with Gandhi's non-violent approach and decided to return to armed resistance. Sanyal found a new generation of college students open to his message. He started recruiting new members in the United Provinces, including Ram Prasad Bismil and Ashfaqullah Khan. He went to Punjab and re-established contact with the surviving Ghadarites, and also visited several colleges. At National College, Lahore, Sanyal

---

[1] Sachindra Nath Sanyal, *Bandi Jeevan*, reprinted in Hindi by Sakshi Prakashan, 2015.

recruited Ajit Singh's talented nephew, Bhagat Singh. The college had been set up recently by Lala Lajpat Rai and Bhai Parmanand as an alternative to government-run colleges. It would prove to be an important recruitment ground for next-generation revolutionaries.

Sanyal reached out to the Anushilan Samiti network in Bengal. This was still the largest revolutionary network in the country but remained divided into numerous semi-independent groups. The Dacca–Barisal group was led by Pratul Ganguli, who was considered the senior-most active leader in Bengal in 1922. Sanyal established contact with him. To improve internal coordination with Sanyal's network, Ganguli sent a young representative, Jogesh Chandra Chatterjee, to Varanasi.

The autobiographical writings by the revolutionaries of this period reflect the fascinating internal debates regarding political strategy. Around this time, Sanyal began to write *Bandi Jeevan*, where he argues that a movement needs poets and writers just as much as it needs warriors and activists. Sanyal wrote his autobiography to inspire a new generation of freedom fighters, but he also specifically mentioned that he wanted to leave behind a first-hand account as he feared that future generations would not be told the truth about the revolutionary movement. This premonition is remarkable in the light of how this history would be edited out in later years.

The Rampa Rebellion[2]

The idea of armed resistance attracted admirers and allies not only in the urban centres but also among rural

---

[2] Compiled from various sources, including K.V. Kurmanath, 'Alluri Sitha Rama Raju: A Folk Hero of Rampa Rebellion', *Heroes of Freedom Struggle-2 series*, Press Information Bureau, Government of India, 9 August 2016, https://pib.gov.in/newsite/printrelease.aspx?relid=148563

peasants and forest tribes. The revolutionary network in the United Provinces began to build close links with one such peasant movement known as the Eka Movement, led by the charismatic Madari Pasi. Barely remembered today, the Eka Movement was a mass peasant movement that ran parallel to the Non-Cooperation Movement. Its leadership was drawn mostly from the lower castes, although its followers included small farmers and farm workers from a range of communities.

Another example of a mass mobilization movement with links to the revolutionaries is the Rampa Rebellion among the forest tribes of the Eastern Ghats in what is now Andhra Pradesh. Its leader was the charismatic Alluri Seetha Rama Raju.

Rama Raju was born in a village near Visakhapatnam in 1897 in a middle-class family. His father, a photographer, died when Rama Raju was still in his teens. The teenager drifted away from formal education, although he was intellectually curious and read extensively in Telugu, Sanskrit and English. He was especially interested in Hindu philosophy. At this time, he also spent time wandering around in the forested hills of the Eastern Ghats, where he became acquainted with the local tribes, particularly the Koya community. This is how he developed a sympathy for their struggles against colonial forest laws and the incursion of Christian missionaries.

Around 1915, when he was about eighteen years old, Rama Raju decided to become a sanyasi (monk) and travelled across India. In Bengal, he met various Anushilan Samiti members and crystallized his ideas of rebellion. He soon decided to return home and start a movement of his own. Like many young activists, Rama Raju was disappointed by the failure of the Non-Cooperation Movement. He began to organize a band of tribesmen to carry out attacks against the colonial administration. Interestingly, they were armed mostly with traditional weapons such as bows and arrows (although they would later add muskets and rifles stolen from the police).

Their first major attack was on the Chintapalli police station in Visakhapatnam district on 22 August 1922. Around 300 tribal warriors joined Rama Raju. This was followed by similar attacks in surrounding areas. The colonial authorities sent in a large number of armed police to counter them, but the rebels were able to evade them easily due to their knowledge of the hilly, forested terrain. Several government troops, including British officers, were killed in the skirmishes. Rama Raju became so confident that he would pre-announce the place and time of his raid, and would leave behind a full list of the things he had taken, one of which was a Webley revolver that he began carrying in his belt.[3]

When the rebellion reached its second year, the British announced a bounty of Rs 10,000 on Rama Raju and Rs 1,000

---

[3] Sumit Bhattacharjee, 'Andhra Pradesh: Alluri Sitharama Raju was first to unite tribal muttas against British, say historians', *The Hindu*, 12 July 2022, https://www.thehindu.com/news/cities/Visakhapatnam/andhra-pradesh-alluri-sitharama-raju-was-first-to-unite-tribal-muttas-against-british-say-historians/article65626873.ece

each for his lieutenants, Ghantam Dora and Mallu Dora. Hundreds of crack troops of the Malabar Special Police and the Assam Rifles were shipped in and put under the command of T.G. Rutherford. Their initial efforts were unsuccessful, as the locals refused to cooperate. They eventually managed to trap Rama Raju near the village of Koyyuru in May 1924. He was tied to a tree and summarily executed by a firing squad. Ghantam Dora was hunted down and killed a month later. Mallu Dora, however, was sent to prison and survived. He would go on to become a Member of Parliament in independent India.

The Constitution of HRA

It is important to understand Sachin Sanyal's aims and objectives at this time. While he was in favour of occasional targeted assassinations of senior British officials, he wanted to create an organization that could coordinate a large-scale armed uprising, followed by the proclamation of an independent republic. The first step was to create an umbrella organization for all the revolutionary groups operating across India.

Thus, Sanyal travelled to Bengal and established contact with various groups. After several rounds of negotiations, Sanyal secretly met Pratul Ganguli and a couple of senior leaders in Bholachang village[4], which is now in Bangladesh. The rebel groups agreed in principle to set up the Hindustan Republican Association (HRA) as an umbrella body with an armed wing called the Hindustan Republican Army.

During the monsoon of 1923, Sanyal made his way in a small country boat to a secret gathering in a remote village

---
[4] Jogesh Chandra Chatterjee, *In Search of Freedom*, published by Paresh Chandra Chatterjee, 1958 (printed by B.K. Majumdar, Calcutta).

near Mymensingh. The fields were flooded and it was possible for the boat to sail right through villages. The meeting was held in a series of interconnected huts built on stilts. All the key revolutionary leaders were present. Sanyal and Ganguli explained the aims and objectives of the HRA. All the groups accepted HRA as the umbrella organization and endorsed Sanyal as the overall leader.

With authority clearly vested in him, Sanyal started to expand and direct the network. Jogesh Chatterjee was told to set up a unit in Kanpur. Bismil and Ashfaqullah were asked to take charge of Shahjahanpur. Jitendra Nath Sanyal, Sachindra Nath Sanyal's younger brother who was working at Indian Press in Allahabad, was put in charge of the city. The youngest brother, Bhupendra Nath Sanyal, still a student, was to assist him. Sachindra Nath Bakshi was initially sent to Lucknow and later to Jhansi. Bhagat Singh was sent to Aligarh, where he was given a job at a new school. A recent recruit, Rajendra Lahiri, was asked to move to Bengal to set up a bomb factory near Dakshineshwar. Jatindra Nath Das, based in Calcutta, functioned as Sanyal's right-hand man.

Meanwhile, in Bengal, the police was on high alert. The colonial authorities were aware that something was afoot and suspected that Pratul Ganguli's Dacca group was involved in it. Realizing that Calcutta and Dacca were too dangerous, Sanyal created a new nerve-centre at Krishnath College in Berhampore where Nalinaksha Sanyal was a lecturer and also the local representative of the Swarajist faction of the INC.

Despite the risks, Sachindra Nath Sanyal decided to shift his base to Bengal, probably to weld the different groups together. The next step was to write out a formal constitution for the HRA. This would not merely lay out the aims and objectives for its members but also pave the way for a future Proclamation of Independence, presumably during an armed uprising. A meeting was held in Kanpur in October 1924, where a draft constitution prepared by Sanyal was debated and adopted in the presence of Rajendra Lahiri, Jogesh Chatterjee, Ram Prasad Bismil and several others.[5]

The HRA constitution prepared by Sanyal is remarkable in that it is the first clear exposition that post-independence India should be a republic based on universal suffrage. The official demand of the INC was still for dominion status (self-government within the British Empire). Gandhi defined the word 'Swaraj' as 'self-government within the Empire if possible—and outside if necessary'.[6] Even those who advocated Purna Swaraj or full independence were not clear what form of government would replace the colonial system. It was the revolutionaries who first enunciated the goal of a fully independent democratic republic.

The HRA constitution soon began to circulate widely and provided a template for setting up local units. Bismil was put in charge of the armed wing. He and/or Sanyal then published a manifesto titled 'The Revolutionary' under a pseudonym, which explained the objectives of the revolutionaries. Copies were printed and distributed widely in many cities across north India on 1 January 1925.

It is interesting to note that the revolutionaries saw themselves not as terrorists or anarchists but as putting up armed resistance to a foreign aggressor. Bismil and/or Sanyal made a clear distinction between the use of targeted violence as resistance and the use of indiscriminate violence to spread fear or an ideology. This was neither violence for the sake of violence, nor was it hatred of the British as a people.

[5] *Ibid.*
[6] Subhas Chandra Bose, *The Indian Struggle*, 1935 (reprinted by Abhishek Publications in 2019).

In February 1925, Sanyal wrote an open letter to Gandhi that was published in *Young India:*

> *You wanted one year for your experiment, but the experiment lasted for at least four complete years, if not five, and still you mean to say that the experiment was not tried long enough? ... To say that non-violent non-cooperation did not work because the people were not sufficiently non-violent is to argue like a lawyer, and not like a prophet. The people could not be more non-violent that they were during the last few years. I would like to say that they were non-violent to a degree that smelt of cowardice.*[7]

The Kakori Train Robbery

Ram Prasad Bismil was born in 1897 into a poor family in a village in Shahjahanpur. By the time he was born, his father had managed to build a small business selling official stamps in the local court. By his own admission, Bismil was an energetic but unruly child, who regularly got into trouble. However, in his mid-teens, he turned to religion and started to conduct the evening rituals at the village temple. He was also influenced by the ideals of the Arya Samaj and a charismatic preacher, Swami Somdev, who strongly advocated nationalist ideas.

The young Bismil's initiation into political life was through the nationalist faction of the Congress. At a party meeting in Lucknow, he organized a small group of volunteers to give Tilak a grand reception, despite opposition from the Loyalist faction. It was also in Lucknow that he first came in contact with the revolutionaries and soon got involved.

[7] As reproduced in Dr C.P. Sharma, *The Builder of Modern India: Bhagat Singh*, Avishkar Prakashan, 2017.

Over the next year, he produced a number of underground pamphlets and posters in support of the freedom struggle; they were all banned by the colonial authorities. In due course, he started to explore ways to acquire small arms.

Like many other revolutionaries, Bismil, too, joined the Non-Cooperation Movement and was deeply disillusioned when it was abruptly withdrawn by Gandhi. It was around this time that he came in contact with Ashfaqullah Khan, who would become his closest friend and chief lieutenant.

When the HRA was formally launched in Kanpur in 1924, Bismil and Ashfaqullah were put in charge of Shahjahanabad. Bismil was also put in charge of the armed wing, which meant that he was responsible for procuring guns. It was no easy task, especially since the revolutionaries were perpetually short of funds. A few sympathetic supporters did provide regular funds, but the growing organization was quickly stripped of resources.

This was clearly not a tenable situation and Bismil began to scout for new sources of funding. In early 1925, the revolutionaries arranged for a talented swimmer, Keshab Chakravarty, to go to Germany for a competition. His real job was to procure a large consignment of Mauser pistols. The pistols were brought by ship to the Bay of Bengal and secretly handed over to Rajendra Lahiri on the high seas outside India's territorial waters.[8]

The need for paying for this large consignment of Mausers added to Bismil's financial urgency. He concluded that raiding the government treasury, although risky, would yield large dividends. Bismil decided to target a train travelling from Saharanpur to Lucknow. He estimated that by the time the train reached Lucknow, the treasury boxes

---

[8] Dharmendra Gaur, *Krantivir Chandrashekhar Azad Aur Unke Do Gaddar Sathi*, reprinted by Bhagat Singh Vichar Manch, Sakshi Prakashan, 2016 (in Hindi).

would contain roughly Rs 10,000, a substantial sum at that time. The plan was to stop the train at Kakori, a small station about 20 kilometres before Lucknow.

Bismil put together a team of ten volunteers. On 9 August 1925, the team boarded the second-class compartment of the train. As planned, the train was brought to a halt using the emergency chain, just outside Kakori station. The guard was forced to the ground while the passengers were instructed to stay calm. A couple of members of the team were assigned to stand along the train and regularly fire into the air to warn off any retaliation. The driver confined himself to his cabin while the engineer locked himself in the toilet. Meanwhile, the steel box containing the money was taken out of the guard's compartment and broken with an axe. They found around Rs 4,600, still a significant sum, and put it into three bags.

Bismil had instructed his men to avoid shooting at anyone unless absolutely necessary. They would later find out that there were fourteen armed persons on the train, including two fully armed soldiers, but none of them fought back. Unfortunately, one unarmed passenger got off the train to see what was happening. He was shot dead in the confusion. Bismil was very upset by this. He admonished the shooter, but it was too late. This shooting converted a robbery into a homicide, a key legal point that the government would use against them later.[9]

Once the money had been taken, the team made their way to Lucknow, where they divided the money and split up. Aside from the single unintended casualty, the raid had been a success. Personal debts were settled and money was set aside for acquiring new weapons. However, the robbery became a media sensation and was reported across the country. The British authorities deployed all available resources to find the culprits.

Soon, some of the stolen currency notes began to circulate and Special Superintendent Horten traced them back to certain locations, including Shahjahanpur. Bismil had not anticipated this flaw in his plan. He was picked up by the police for questioning. Banarasi Lal, a member of the network, was arrested from Rae Baraeli and cracked during interrogation and revealed details of the entire HRA network.

Armed with this information, the police arrested people across the country, including those not directly linked to the robbery. In Dakshineshwar, Rajendra Lahiri was arrested after the police found one live bomb, seven revolvers, one pistol, anti-British literature and supplies for making explosives. Sachindra Nath Sanyal and his youngest brother Bhupendra

---

[9] Ram Prasad Bismil, *The Revolutionary,* translated and edited by Saket Suryesh, Notion Press, 2020.

Nath were also arrested. Ashfaqullah managed to evade arrest for some time, but was eventually caught.

The Kakori Conspiracy Case dragged on for a year and garnered a lot of media attention. The Swarajist faction of the INC even organized a defence team. Thirty-one persons were tried. There were some daring attempts to escape. Sachindra Nath Sanyal's other brother, Rabindra, who had not been arrested, managed to smuggle in a hacksaw inside a copy of the Tulsi Ramayan. Sanyal nearly escaped by cutting through the iron bars but was caught, mercilessly beaten and put in solitary confinement.[10] Similarly, a hacksaw was smuggled to Bismil. He managed to get out of his cell with two others, but was unable to scale the walls undetected.

Even as they waited for the verdict in the spring of 1927, Bismil composed the famous revolutionary song *Mera Range De Basanti Chola*—and all the other prisoners began to sing along. The lyrics found their way out of the prison

दम निकले इस देश की खातिर
बस इतना अरमान है
एक बार इस राह में मरना
सौ जन्मों के समान है
देख के वीरों की कुरबानी
अपना दिल भी बोला
ओ मेरा रंग दे बसंती चोला ओये
रंग दे बसंती चोला
माये रंग दे बसंती चोला

---

[10] Rabindranath Sanyal, *Reminiscences of Rabindra Nath Sanyal: Essays written in memory of Shahid Sachindra Nath Sanyal*, 1983.

and soon became a popular anthem. The verdict was read out at Lucknow's Ring Theatre amid elaborate security arrangements. Ram Prasad Bismil, Thakur Roshan Singh, Ashfaqullah Khan and Rajendra Lahiri were sentenced to death; Sachindra Nath Sanyal, Jogesh Chatterjee and two others were given transportation for life and a dozen more, including Bhupendra Nath Sanyal, were given sentences ranging from five to fourteen years. There were widespread protests against the sentences and the elected members of the UP Legislative Council passed a resolution asking the government to at least commute capital punishment to life imprisonment. Madan Mohan Malaviya even met the viceroy to push for reduced sentences. But the government did not budge.

Bismil spent his last days writing his autobiography—*The Revolutionary*. He was hanged on 18 December 1927. His last words were: 'I wish the downfall of the British Empire.' Roshan Singh and Rajendra Lahiri bravely walked up to the gallows holding a copy of the Bhagawad Gita and singing *Vande Mataram*. Ashfaqullah went to his death with a Quran tied around his neck. At the end, he said, 'I tried to make India free, and the attempt will not end with my life.' He then smiled.[11]

The Sanyal family was devastated by the Kakori sentences—Bhupendra Nath was imprisoned for five years, while Sachindra Nath was sent back to Port Blair for life, the only person to have been sent to the dreaded Cellular Jail twice. All the ancestral properties of the extended clan in Varanasi were either confiscated or forcibly acquired. A few reminders of the times can still be seen at Bengali Tola Intercollege, which has plaques for founders and freedom fighters that bear the names of several generations of the

---

[11] *Struggle for Freedom*, edited by R.C. Majumdar, Bharatiya Vidya Bhavan, 1969 (reprinted in 1979).

family. There is also the house of Sachindra Nath Sanyal's granduncle, the famous yogi Lahiri Mahashaya, which continues to be a shrine to the saint.

Regrouping after Kakori

The Kakori arrests and the sustained raids against the Anushilan Samiti groups in Bengal had severely depleted the senior leadership of the HRA by 1926. This left the surviving network in the hands of an even younger group of activists, which included Sukhdev Thapar, Bhagat Singh and Chandrashekhar Azad. When they assumed control of the organization, Azad was barely twenty years old and the other two just nineteen!

Chandra Shekhar Tiwari was born in 1906 in a poor Brahmin family in Bhabhra village in the small princely state of Alirajpur, now part of Madhya Pradesh. Like Bismil, Azad was a restless teenager and, at the age of fourteen, left his village for Bombay. He knew no one in the city and earned a living by washing dishes in a restaurant and then working at the docks as a ship painter. It was hard work, but it gave him a wider view of the world. After a year or so, he decided on a whim to accompany a co-worker to Varanasi. Here he enrolled himself at a Sanskrit pathshala. The school provided meals and a place to stay and also introduced him to the charged political milieu of Varanasi.

Like many other students in the city, Chandra Shekhar also participated in a number of protests during the Non-Cooperation Movement and was arrested. When produced before the magistrate, he was asked his name and replied 'Azad', meaning 'free'. This is how he ended up with this moniker. The magistrate was not amused and awarded him fifteen strokes of the cane. Azad bore the punishment without flinching, crying out 'Vande Mataram' at each stroke. The news of his bravery soon spread and was reported in some Indian-language papers. Thus, Azad became a minor celebrity.[12]

By 1923, Sachindra Nath Sanyal had established a hub in Varanasi that operated clandestinely out of a religious institution called Kalyan Ashram. Rajendra Lahiri was the key organizer of operations in the city and it was he who recruited Azad. Over the next two years, the teenage revolutionary played a minor part in the activities of the newly formed HRA.

The arrests following the Kakori incident threw the organization into turmoil. Azad escaped to Jhansi, where he lived for a while working as a car mechanic and then as a sadhu in a forest temple.

It was clear by mid-1927 that the HRA needed new leadership as most of the experienced revolutionaries had been killed, were on death row or in jail with long sentences. Azad travelled to Maharashtra to meet Vinayak Savarkar for guidance. Savarkar had been freed from jail with severe restrictions and was under constant surveillance. It was a risky meeting for both of them. Azad came away inspired by the veteran and threw himself into building a new network. One of first things he did was garner funds. There is evidence that many leading figures of that time contributed money to the cause, including Motilal Nehru, Purushottam Das Tandon and the writer Sarat Chandra Chatterjee.[13]

One of Azad's key allies in this rebuilding effort was Bhagat Singh. He was born in 1907 in the village of Banga in the Lyallpur district of Punjab (now in Pakistan) into a family

[12] Dharmendra Gaur, *Krantivir Chandrashekhar Azad Aur Unke Do Gaddar Sathi*, reprinted by Bhagat Singh Vichar Manch, Sakshi Prakashan, 2016 (in Hindi).
[13] *Ibid.*

Bhagat Singh

d. 23 March 1931, 23 years
LAHORE
BANGA
b. 28 September 1907

of wealthy landowners closely associated with the Arya Samaj movement. After matriculation, he joined the National College in Lahore, which had been newly established by Lala Lajpat Rai and Bhai Parmanand. It was in college that he met other young men who dreamt of an armed insurrection against the British. The Non-Cooperation Movement had collapsed and the disillusioned youth of Punjab were open to Sachindra Nath Sanyal's ideas when he visited Lahore during 1922–24.

After joining the organization, Bhagat Singh spent some time in Allahabad, Kanpur and Aligarh. Like Azad, Bhagat Singh was left a political orphan after the Kakori arrests and decided to return to Punjab. In October 1926, a bomb was thrown at a Ram Leela procession in Lahore, killing many, including children. The police blamed it on the revolutionaries and arrested Bhagat Singh. He was later freed for lack of evidence, but it shows that he was already being watched. It was during this period that he began to read more about Marxism. There was little literature available on the topic until the late twenties, and few Indians had a clear idea of the Marxist frame of thinking. Bhagat Singh was among the first in India to take an interest in Marxist ideas.

From the middle of 1927, the revolutionaries began to regroup. A clandestine meeting of the surviving units took place in Kanpur in July 1928. The groups in Punjab and the United Provinces were keen to re-establish a centralized leadership, but the groups in Bengal disagreed. Thus, the Bengal revolutionaries kept away from the second meeting, which took place in September 1928 in the medieval ruins of Ferozeshah Kotla in Delhi. A central leadership was constituted with two members each from Punjab, the United Provinces and Bihar, and one from Rajputana (Rajasthan). There was no representative from Bengal. Azad, who was not present, was unanimously elected as head of the armed wing. This effectively made him the senior-most leader of this generation of revolutionaries. At this meeting, Bhagat Singh also proposed a change of name to Hindustan Socialist Republican Association (HSRA), which was ultimately accepted.

Avenging Lala Lajpat Rai

The Government of India Act of 1919 had a provision that required political reforms and greater representation of Indians to be reviewed after ten years. However, the British establishment feared that a Labour government might offer too many concessions to the Indians. Thus, rather in a hurry, a commission was announced under the chairmanship of Sir John Simon. It included seven British members of Parliament and had no Indian representation.

Not surprisingly, the commission faced stiff opposition from Indians from the very start. When the commission travelled to India in 1928, it was met with vociferous protests at every location. Large processions marched through major cities, carrying black flags and banners stating 'Go Back, Simon'. Expatriate Indians also organized protests across the world.

On 30 October, the Simon Commission faced a large gathering of protesters led by Lala Lajpat Rai in Lahore. A large police contingent pushed them back. In an impromptu speech, Lajpat Rai mocked the government: *'If the government did not wish the Commission to see the demonstrators, the best thing for it to do was to put blindfolds over the eyes of the members and take them straight to Government House.'* As tempers rose, the Superintendent of Police James Scott ordered a lathi charge. The crowd initially dispersed, but on seeing Lajpat Rai standing alone, they came back in force. Scott decided to target the leader, and a group of policemen led by Scott beat him mercilessly. They kept hitting Lajpat Rai on the head until he collapsed, bleeding profusely. All this was done in full public view, as the purpose was to instil fear. There is evidence that Bhagat Singh witnessed the event.[14]

---

[14] Multiple sources, including Kuldip Nayar, *Without Fear: The Life and Trial of Bhagat Singh*, HarperCollins India, 2012; Dharmendra Gaur, *Krantivir Chandrashekhar Azad Aur Unke Do Gaddar Sathi*, reprinted by Bhagat Singh Vichar Manch, Sakshi Prakashan, 2016 (in Hindi); and Jitendra Nath Sanyal, *Bhagat Singh: A Biography*, reprinted by Hope India Publications, 2014.

Lala Lajpat Rai never recovered from the injuries and died on 17 November 1928. His death sent shock waves across India. He was no ordinary leader, but had been at the forefront of the freedom movement for three decades. The repeated use of lethal force against unarmed protesters ignited public opinion. On 10 December, key revolutionaries, including Shivaram Rajguru, Bhagat Singh, Sukhdev Thapar and Chandrashekhar Azad, met in Lahore in the house of Bhagwati Charan Vohra. Vohra was away in Calcutta, but his wife, Durga Devi (affectionately called Durga Bhabi), played host. The revolutionaries unanimously decided to kill Scott to send a message that violence would be met with violence.

Sukhdev was given the role of mission planner. He chose Rajguru, Bhagat Singh, Jai Gopal and Azad for the task. The date was fixed for 17 December 1928. Each member was given a role: Bhagat Singh was to shoot Scott, Rajguru was to provide covering fire and Azad was to cover the escape. Jai Gopal, the junior-most member of the team, was to keep a lookout and let the others know that Scott had arrived at the police station. He was not part of the main operation.

Over the next few days, the revolutionaries scouted the location. It was decided that the Dayanand Anglo Vedic (DAV) College provided the best escape route.

As it happened, Scott did not come to the police station on 17 December. Jai Gopal mistook Assistant Superintendent John Saunders for Scott and informed the waiting team. Saunders had also been involved in directing the lathi charge on the protesters, but it is not clear whether he was involved in beating up Lajpat Rai. When Saunders came out of the premises in the afternoon, Bhagat Singh realized they had the wrong man. However, Rajguru had already pulled out his Mauser and opened fire. Bhagat Singh also shot at the police officer before they ran towards the college. Another British officer, Inspector W.J.C. Fern, came out to see what was happening but ran back in when Azad shot at him. Only the head constable, Chanan Singh, gave chase. The revolutionaries begged him to turn back as they did not want to spill Indian blood, but when he kept running after them, Rajguru shot him dead. Several people witnessed the shootings, including the famed Urdu poet Faiz Ahmad Faiz.

The three revolutionaries now ran into DAV College, scaled the walls and went into the hostel. Here they picked up their bicycles and left immediately. The police later surrounded and ransacked the college premises, but it was soon obvious that they had escaped.

Holed up in their hideout on Mozang Road, the three revolutionaries knew that the police was systematically combing the city and would eventually knock on their door. They needed to get out of Lahore. They made their way before dawn to Durga Devi's house to consult with her and Sukhdev. It was decided that they would leave that very day for Calcutta, with Bhagat Singh and Durga Devi disguised as a well-to-do couple—Ranjit and Sujata. Her three-year-old son would be their child and Rajguru would act as their servant. Azad opted to make separate arrangements.

Dressed in European clothes, including an overcoat and a felt hat, Ranjit walked confidently into Lahore station. He was accompanied by his well-dressed wife and followed by a servant, dressed in old clothes, carrying a child. The station was being closely watched, but no one suspected the family that walked into the first-class compartment. Having settled them in, the loyal servant went to his seat in the third-class compartment. Unknown to them, Azad was on the same train as a member of a party of pilgrims headed for Mathura. Bhagat Singh and Durga Devi changed trains at Lucknow for Calcutta as the police in Bengal was keeping a close watch on direct trains from Lahore, and safely reached Calcutta.

Bombing the Assembly

Once the initial furore over the Saunders killing had died down, the revolutionaries rented two small houses in Agra's Hing ki Mandi, which became the new headquarters for Azad, Bhagat, Sukhdev and Rajguru. They were soon joined by a number of new recruits as well as old HRA activists from the pre-Kakori years—Jatindra Nath Das (shortened henceforth to Jatin Das), Batukeshwar Dutt and Ram Saran Das. Jatin Das had been Sachindra Nath Sanyal's key lieutenant during his stint in Calcutta and was an explosives expert. Batukeshwar was from Bengal but had been recruited when he was studying in Kanpur. Ram Saran had been sentenced in the Kakori case and had recently returned after serving a sentence in the Cellular Jail.

The revolutionaries, as usual, were desperately short of funds but they would occasionally receive help from the strangest of sources. For example, Azad once received a bearer cheque from Bengal's advocate general Sir N. Sircar. Azad immediately had it encashed so as to leave no trace.

In early 1929, Viceroy Irwin introduced two bills for discussion. The first, the Public Safety Bill, was designed to empower the government to detain anyone without trial. The second, the Trade Disputes Bill, was designed to deter trade unions from going on strike. The revolutionaries decided that they would express their opposition to these laws by throwing a bomb in the Central Legislative Assembly in Delhi on 8 April, when the bills were to be debated. The idea was not to hurt anyone but to attract public attention. Unlike in the Saunders assassination, the activists would make no attempt to escape but would court arrest to make a strong statement.

Batukeshwar Dutt and Ram Saran Das were initially chosen to carry out the operation. However, an argument arose between Sukhdev and Bhagat Singh, where the former accused the latter of being too cowardly to do it himself. This stung Bhagat Singh and he now insisted on leading the mission. Azad realized that this was a bad idea as it could lead the police to work out his link to the Saunders killing. The throwing of a non-lethal bomb would result in a prison term, but the killing of a police officer meant capital punishment. Unfortunately, Bhagat Singh was adamant.

On the morning of 8 April, Durga Devi, Bhagwati Charan and Azad met Bhagat Singh for a 'picnic' in Qudsia Park in Old Delhi. Few words were exchanged as Bhagat Singh ate oranges and his favourite sweets. Everyone knew that this would be the last time he would be free.[15]

Bhagat Singh left the park and headed for the Central Legislative Assembly building, where Batukeshwar was waiting for him. They were dressed in khaki shorts and shirts. An Indian member gave them passes at the entrance and then disappeared into the crowd. A few minutes before 11 a.m., the two made their way into the crowded public gallery. They could see many well-known people below—Motilal Nehru, M.A. Jinnah, Madan Mohan Malaviya and even Sir John Simon. Bhagat Singh carefully threw his bomb away from the seated members. The explosion led to utter confusion. Then

[15] Kama Maclean, *A Revolutionary History of Interwar India*, Penguin India, 2015.

a second bomb thrown by Batukeshwar exploded, followed by a shower of leaflets. The low-intensity bombs were designed to be loud rather than deadly, but pandemonium broke out as people rushed in panic for the doors.

The two revolutionaries had fully loaded revolvers and could have killed several officials if they had wished. But they calmly put down the revolvers on adjoining chairs when the police arrived. Even as they were arrested, they shouted, 'Long Live the Revolution' and 'Down with Imperialism'. The idea was to make a political statement and the leaflets made the point, quoting Auguste Vaillant: *'It takes a loud voice to make the deaf hear.'*

The British were aware that the revolutionaries intended to use the attack to stir up public opinion. Hence, the police instructed the press to play down the events. Most papers initially complied but *Hindustan Times* ran the story prominently. The chairman of the newspaper, Madan Mohan Malaviya, publicly maintained a distance from the revolutionaries but employed several journalists who were sympathetic to their cause. While the editorials carefully toed the government line, the story was given full front-page coverage on 10 April. Other papers followed suit.[16]

A few days later, photographs of the two revolutionaries were released. This included the well-known image of Bhagat Singh wearing a hat. Within a few days, the images spread across India and began to be reproduced both in mainstream newspapers and underground publications. Bhagat Singh's cool hat made him instantly recognizable, and it became what would be today called a viral meme. Batukeshwar's dreamy, boyish look elicited a lot of sympathy. The two of them became instant national heroes.

[16] *Ibid.*

Meanwhile, the British suspected that Bhagat Singh was involved in the Saunders killing. A special investigation was initiated to look into possible links between the events in Lahore and Delhi. The trial for the Assembly Bombing Case began a few weeks later under unprecedented security. The two defendants were unfazed and kept interrupting the proceedings by shouting slogans. Bhagat Singh even took a dig at Gandhi: '*We have only marked the end of the era of utopian non-violence, of whose futility the rising generation has been convinced beyond the shadow of doubt.*'[17] After a show trial, both of them were sentenced to fourteen years in jail.

British officials, however, were not satisfied as they wanted to establish who had killed Saunders and shut down the wider network. The number of police raids in Lahore increased and several suspected HSRA members were arrested. One of them, Jai Gopal, agreed to turn approver. This was a major breakthrough as he revealed the names of the others. Hans Raj, a new recruit who had helped make the posters, turned approver a few days later. Based on information from the two, Sukhdev, Rajguru, Jatin Das and several others were caught and brought to Lahore. One of Sachindra Nath Sanyal's brothers, Jitendra Nath, was also arrested. He would later write an underground biography of Bhagat Singh, published in 1931, that provides a valuable eye-witness account of what followed.[18]

---

[17] *Ibid.*
[18] Jitendra Nath Sanyal, *Bhagat Singh: A Biography,* reprinted by Hope India Publications, 2014.

The Second Lahore Conspiracy Case

The trial began in the intense heat of May 1930. It is now remembered as the Second Lahore Conspiracy Case, not to be confused with the First Lahore Conspiracy Case of 1915 involving the Ghadarite generation of revolutionaries. In the audience was Bhagat Singh's father Kishan Singh, who, despite his son's objections, had constituted a defence team. It must have been quite a moment when the prisoners entered together, singing *'Sarfaroshi ki tamanna ab hamare dil mein hai ...',* a song popularized by Bismil, which means 'The dream of self-sacrifice now fills our hearts'. Many members of the audience began to sing along.[19]

The judges had only just managed to re-establish order when Rajguru stood up and stated that the viceroy did not have the authority to try them by a special tribunal and that the trial was invalid. This was followed by a statement read out by Jitendra Nath Sanyal on behalf of the prisoners. The statement, co-authored with Bhagat Singh, argued that the defenders of India's honour and freedom could not be tried as criminals. Given the crimes against humanity committed by the British, it was the colonial administration that should be put on trial.

For the next several days, the prisoners were brought to the court, but the trial could not proceed as the accused would either shout slogans or sing. Eventually, the two British judges, Coldstream and Hilton, asked the police to use force. The police entered the box and mercilessly beat the prisoners. There was utter pandemonium in the court as the accused were dragged away. Agha Haider, the only Indian member of the tribunal, made a statement disassociating himself from

---

[19] Kuldip Nayar, *Without Fear: The Life and Trial of Bhagat Singh*, HarperCollins India, 2012.

the actions of the police. The revolutionaries henceforth boycotted the trial and the tribunal had to proceed without them. All of this was widely covered in the press and had the whole country riveted.

Even as the courtroom drama was playing itself out, Azad and Bhagwati Charan were at large. In mid-December, a team led by Bhagwati Charan rigged explosives to the railway tracks entering Delhi from the south, not far from Purana Qila. Then they waited for the viceroy's special train that was supposed to pass this section on 23 December. A mid-level HSRA member, Yashpal, was given the job of pressing the switch. Unfortunately, the trigger was mistimed and the explosion took place a few seconds after the viceroy's carriage had passed. The viceroy was unhurt, although the explosion caused extensive damage to some of the other bogies.

Undeterred by the failed attack, Azad and Bhagwati Charan started planning a daring attempt to free their comrades. The date was set for 1 June 1930, when Bhagat Singh and Batukeshwar Dutt were supposed to be taken from Central Jail to Borstal Jail. Two teams were set up to carry out the operation at the gates of Borstal Jail. Unfortunately, the plan went horribly wrong when Bhagwati Charan was killed as a bomb went off accidentally during the preparations. Whatever her internal turmoil, Durga Devi was outwardly stoical about the death of her husband and remained an active member of the movement.

The tribunal delivered its judgment on 7 October 1930. Bhagat Singh, Sukhdev Thapar and Shivaram Rajguru were sentenced to death by hanging; eight others were sentenced to long jail terms. Jitendra Nath Sanyal and two others were freed for lack of evidence.

The hangings were scheduled for 24 March 1931. There was a lot of pressure on Gandhi to push for clemency during his extensive meetings with Viceroy Irwin in the first week of March. To this day, there is much debate over whether Gandhi did indeed discuss the matter with the viceroy. The best available evidence suggests that he briefly raised the matter but did not press it, and there is a possibility that he was subtly misled by the viceroy to believe that the executions were not imminent.[20]

Bhagat Singh, Sukhdev and Rajguru were hanged on 23 March, a day ahead of schedule. The bodies were then smuggled out in sacks by the police through a hole in the back wall of the jail and secretly burnt on the banks of the Sutlej in Hussainiwala. The local villagers found the half-burnt remains and cremated them properly a day later. News of the hangings cast a pall of gloom over the country.

The place where the three were cremated ended up in Pakistan after Partition, but was taken back by India in 1961 in exchange for twelve villages. A National Martyrs' Memorial was built in 1968, but was ransacked by Pakistani armoured units during the war of 1971. The memorial was rebuilt in 1973.[21]

The Battle of Alfred Park

After the death of Bhagwati Charan and the announcement of the sentences in Lahore, Azad, left almost alone, carried on travelling across north India to keep the network going. In early 1931, he moved to Allahabad and started operating from a house in the Katra area of the city. A few HSRA members, including Durga Devi and Yashpal, met him there to discuss

---

[20] Multiple sources, including Kuldip Nayar, *Without Fear: The Life and Trial of Bhagat Singh*, HarperCollins India, 2012; and Jitendra Nath Sanyal, *Bhagat Singh: A Biography*, reprinted by Hope India Publications, 2014.

[21] Anirudh Gupta, 'Nationalism's forgotten corner', *The Tribune*, 14 August, https://www.tribuneindia.com/news/archive/punjab/nationalism-s-forgotten-corner-637570

the future course of action. Sachindra Nath Sanyal was in Cellular Jail at this time, but his extended family had moved to Allahabad. His wife Pratibha and brother Rabindra Nath were aware that Azad was in the city.

There is evidence that Azad and Yashpal met Jawaharlal Nehru around 20 February. Motilal Nehru had passed away just days earlier. Since he had been supportive of the revolutionary cause in his later years, it is likely that Azad wanted to convey his condolences as well as elicit some help. Yashpal later claimed that the meeting did not go well, as Jawaharlal was generally dismissive of the revolutionary approach. Jawaharlal also briefly recalled the incident in the first edition of his autobiography.[22] Curiously, he dropped it in later editions.

On the morning of 27 February, Rabindra Nath Sanyal was teaching a niece at his house when he noticed a large number of plain-clothes policemen in the street below.[23] Long accustomed to being under surveillance, he knew that something was afoot and wondered how to warn Azad, who was expected to drop in that day.

A stone's throw away, in Alfred Park, Azad and Sukhdev Raj were casually walking towards the Indian Press gate. They had spotted an old comrade, Veerbhadra Tiwari, a few minutes earlier. Veerbhadra had been arrested for the Kakori case but had escaped punishment. He had re-established contact with the revolutionaries, but Azad had kept him at arm's length. Suddenly seeing him in Allahabad made Azad suspicious. Sukhdev and Azad were still in conversation when they saw an armed police officer, Visheshwar Singh, enter the park along with another policeman and walk past them. Clearly something was going on.

---

[22] Kama Maclean, *A Revolutionary History of Interwar India*, Penguin India, 2015.
[23] As an aside, the niece's son, Shyamal Dev Goswamy, would be awarded the Mahavir Chakra for bravery during the Indo-China War of 1962.

Suddenly, a car came to a halt and the city's crime branch chief, John Nott-Bower, jumped out. He asked the two men to put their hands up. Azad pulled out his pistol and shot out the car's tyres, but was shot by Nott-Bower in the thigh. Sukhdev and Azad now ran into the park and hid behind a jamun tree. By this time, Visheshwar Singh and several other armed policemen had taken up positions and were firing at them.

Azad realized that he could not escape with a badly injured leg. He ordered Sukhdev to escape while he provided covering fire. The gunfight lasted for quite some time. Visheshwar Singh was hit in the jaw while Nott-Bower was hit in the wrist. Azad was a good shot and the police could not get closer, but he was surrounded, injured and running out of ammunition. When he had only one bullet left, he shot himself through the head, thus keeping his promise that he would never be taken alive.

A few hundred metres away, the Sanyal household listened to the gunfight in horror. Once the shooting had died down, Rabindra Nath and Pratibha carefully made their way to Alfred Park. The police cordon did not allow them to get close, but they could recognize their comrade's body in the distance. The colonial administration was aware that Azad's heroic last stand had made him a potent martyr. The body was hurriedly taken to the river and cremated. However, senior Congress leader Purushottam Das Tandon arrived in time to witness the cremation and collect the ashes. He then took the ashes into the city, where a meeting had been organized by the Allahabad Students' Association. Kamala Nehru and Pratibha Sanyal addressed an emotionally charged audience. Several students smeared Azad's ashes on their forehead and swore that they would avenge his death.

◆ 7 ◆
CHITTAGONG

EVEN AS THESE dramatic events were playing out in Lahore and Allahabad, the revolutionaries in Bengal had not been quiet. Following the arrests of senior leaders in the mid-1920s, a new generation had emerged here as well. Perhaps the most charismatic of these leaders was Surya Sen.[1] He was born in 1894 in Chittagong (now Chattogram in Bangladesh). He was initiated into the world of the revolutionaries while an undergraduate at Krishnath College in Berhampore, a hotbed of the Jugantar group.

Surya Sen returned to Chittagong and became a mathematics teacher at National High School. This is why he came to be known widely as 'Master-da' (schoolmaster). The Easter Rebellion in Ireland in April 1916 had a deep impact on him and he planned to instigate a similar revolt in India. In the early 1920s, Sen was part of the Anushilan Samiti network in east Bengal and was witness to the formation of the HRA as an umbrella body. However, like most Bengali groups, his unit did not join the HSRA when it was reconstituted by Azad and Bhagat Singh. Instead, the eastern-most wing of the HRA was rebranded as the Indian Republican Army. It is unclear why it opted for this name, but it is possible that it was done simply to acquire the same acronym as the Irish Republican Army.

The Armoury Raid

On the morning of 18 April 1930, Good Friday, the Indian Republican Army struck in Chittagong. Around 10 a.m., an advance party hijacked two taxis and attacked the telegraph

---

[1] Multiple sources, including Uma Mukherjee, *Two Great Revolutionaries,* Dey's Publishing, 2004; Subodh Roy, *Chittagong Armoury Raid: A Memoir,* Leftword, 2015; Jalad Baran Das, *Hijli Detention Camp to IIT: An Untold Saga,* Nehru Museum of Science & Technology, 2009.

office and telephone exchange to sever communication with the rest of the world. Meanwhile, the main activists, dressed in khaki, raided the police armoury. The revolutionaries only had a few pistols among them, but they took the police completely by surprise. The same thing happened at the auxiliary forces armoury. The rebels then collected rifles and a couple of machine guns from the armoury but could not find the appropriate ammunition. Thus, they had to be satisfied with smooth-bore muskets. These were single-shot guns with relatively poor range, but they had no choice.

One party was sent to the local European club to look for any officials who might be there, but found it empty. Another chased away a group of Europeans who had organized a response team with weapons from the Chittagong port armoury. Nonetheless, it was obvious to the leaders, Surya Sen and Ganesh Ghosh, that they could not hold the town for long with barely fifty-six men armed with muskets. They decided to head into the hills.

For the next three days, Surya Sen led his men further into the hills. They were desperately hungry and thirsty, and weighed down by guns and ammunition. Some sympathetic villagers provided them with meals along the way, but they could not linger anywhere for too long. They knew that the British administration would have restored communication by now and would be looking for them. On more than one occasion, they saw a plane flying low over them.[2]

On 22 April, the group took up positions on a hillock known as Jalalabad. It was around 5 p.m. when they saw a large number of government troops gathering some distance away. The troops tried to encircle the hillock. The British officers planning the assault might have felt that the

[2] Subodh Roy, *Chittagong Armory Raid: A Memoir*, Leftword, 2015.

revolutionaries would realize their impossible situation and quickly capitulate. They were probably also encouraged by the lack of response as they closed in. However, recognizing the limitations of the muskets, Surya Sen had ordered his men to hold their fire until the enemy was very close. Then, all of a sudden, the revolutionaries opened a volley at close quarters. The government troops were forced to fall back, with several casualties. This was followed by a few more waves of frontal assault with the same result. The British now withdrew and positioned some machine guns on a hill that overlooked Jalalabad. From here, they kept up constant fire that proved more effective. Several revolutionaries were killed at this stage.

As it became dark, the revolutionaries realized that firing from the opposite side had stopped. Surya Sen and the surviving men used the opportunity to escape. A later statement by Charles Tegart, Calcutta police commissioner, suggests that twelve revolutionaries died on Jalalabad hill while the government lost sixty-four men. This was quite a performance by a ragtag group against well-armed professionals.[3] Surya Sen remained at large and kept directing guerrilla attacks until he was betrayed and captured in February 1933. He was hanged a year later.

The Chittagong armoury raid was never going to succeed as a military operation. All the participants knew this. The objective was to inspire a wave of unrest—and it succeeded. In the next two years, Bengal saw a large number of attacks on government officials, which paralysed the colonial administration. On 25 August 1930, Tegart narrowly escaped death when Dinesh Majumdar and Anuj Sen threw a bomb at his car. Dinesh escaped but Anuj was killed in the encounter.

[3] *Ibid.*

Four days later, Benoy Basu shot dead Inspector General Lowman in Dacca. He escaped in disguise from Dacca and headed to Calcutta, where he planned an even more audacious attack.

On 8 December, Benoy Basu, Badal Gupta and Dinesh Gupta entered Writers' Building, the secretariat, and shot dead Inspector General of Prisons J.J. Simpson. This was followed by a famous gunfight in the corridors of the secretariat, remembered as the 'Battle of the Verandah'. Benoy and Badal shot themselves with their last bullets while Dinesh was hanged in 1931. Dalhousie Square—the open area in front of Writers' Building—is today known as Benoy–Badal–Dinesh Bagh in their memory.

Even as political violence in the rest of Bengal increased, the district magistrate of Midnapur, James Peddie, ordered the police to shoot down peasants refusing to pay taxes. The revolutionaries not only killed him but two of his successors as well.[4] Inevitably, the British responded by arresting those suspected of links with the revolutionaries. Many of them were housed in a new detention centre at Hijli in Midnapur.

On 27 July 1931, J.J. Garlicks, the sessions judge who had sentenced Dinesh Gupta to death, was shot dead by the revolutionaries. This news was reportedly received with jubilation by the inmates at Hijli. The authorities were even more enraged when three inmates escaped. They decided to teach the inmates a lesson and, on the night of 16 September 1931, fifty armed guards entered the facility and fired at the prisoners. Two of the inmates died and twenty-nine were badly injured.[5]

News of the attack on the unarmed inmates soon leaked out and caused public outrage. Subhas Chandra Bose visited Hijli to collect the bodies of the martyrs. Many prominent Indians, including Rabindranath Tagore, condemned the government. Political prisoners across Bengal went on hunger strike, demanding an inquiry. The government inquiry concluded: 'In our opinion, there is no proper justification for the indiscriminate firing by the sepoys at the Detention Camp which killed two political prisoners and injured many others.'[6]

Following the Hijli incident, the authorities began to monitor Subhas Bose's links with the revolutionaries with renewed suspicion. Not only was Bose showing a great deal of public sympathy for the martyrs, some of the new breed of revolutionaries were also found to have links with the Bengal Volunteers, which had been set up by Bose for the Calcutta

---
[4] Sugata Bose, *His Majesty's Opponent*, Penguin India, 2013.
[5] Jalad Baran Das, *Hijli Detention Camp to IIT: An Untold Saga*, Nehru Museum of Science & Technology, 2009.
[6] *Ibid.*

session of the INC in 1928 as an organizing corps for the event. However, it subsequently developed a life of its own. The trio that attacked Writers' Building, for instance, had links with the organization.

> In February 1932, a revolutionary named Bina Das attempted to shoot Bengal Governor Stanley Jackson in the convocation hall of Calcutta University. She fired five shots but missed, and was sentenced to nine years in prison.

This sharp escalation of revolutionary activity across India, however, lost steam by 1933. Almost all key leaders had been either killed or imprisoned. Despite his sympathies for the revolutionary cause, Subhas Bose was not yet ready to pick up the leadership under these circumstances. Thus, there was a lull for a period of about six years in the mainstream revolutionary movement. This was a period when the Communist Party of India and the Rashtriya Swayamsevak Sangh (RSS) emerged. Both of them were started by survivors from the insurrection attempts during the First World War.

The Many Adventures of M.N. Roy

Some think that the communist movement in India began with Bhagat Singh. However, the real founder of the Communist Party of India is another fascinating character—Manabendra Nath Roy, or M.N. Roy.

He was born as Narendra Nath Bhattacharya in Bengal in 1887, and joined the Anushilan Samiti during the protests against the Partition of Bengal in 1905.[7] After the arrest of Aurobindo and Barin Ghosh, he drifted into Bagha Jatin's

---

[7] *Selected Works of M.N. Roy Volume I: 1917-1922*, edited by Sibnarayan Ray, Oxford University Press, 1987.

Jugantar group. He had been part of the meeting that had planned the Rodda arms heist, but had opted out as he felt it was too risky. When Bagha Jatin was negotiating with the Germans for a large arms consignment in 1915, he sent Narendra to Batavia (now Jakarta) to coordinate the logistics with the German consul-general. However, the consignment never reached India and Bagha Jatin was killed while waiting for it on the Balasore coast. The British then proceeded to arrest many members of the Jugantar group. Thus, Narendra found himself stranded in Southeast Asia.

Unsure of what to do next, he decided to go to California in the hope of joining the Ghadarite community. He also changed his name to M.N. Roy to throw British intelligence off his scent. Here he met and married Evelyn Trent, a graduate student at Stanford University with a passion for radical politics. The United States joined the war in 1917, and it immediately became a dangerous place for Indians with revolutionary links. So, Roy and his wife escaped to Mexico, where Roy met Michael Borodin and together with him founded the Communist Party of Mexico in 1919.

On Borodin's recommendation, Roy was invited to Moscow to meet Lenin. By all accounts, Roy impressed Lenin and was given access to the top Soviet leadership. He was then sent to Tashkent with orders to set up a Marxist indoctrination school for Indians. Several Indian activists had sought refuge in the Soviet Union after the Turko-German alliance surrendered. Lenin wanted to use them to create a group steeped in Bolshevik ideas, which could be deployed to pressure the British in India when necessary. This is how the Communist Party of India (CPI) was founded in Tashkent on 17 October 1920.

M.N. Roy was not very successful in spreading communism in India. The British arrested most of the indoctrinated groups that were sent back to the country, and the individuals who evaded arrest showed little interest in spreading the message. Nonetheless, the colonial authorities issued a warrant against him in 1924.

When Stalin grabbed power after Lenin's death, Roy found that he no longer had a sympathetic supporter. Roy quietly left Moscow for Berlin in April 1929 and returned to India in December 1930. He was already in touch with some senior leaders and, on the invitation of Jawaharlal Nehru, he secretly attended the Karachi session of the Congress. The police eventually traced him to a house in Bombay and arrested him on the basis of the warrant of 1924. He was sentenced to twelve years in prison.[8]

Meanwhile, the CPI was finally gaining some traction. Ironically, this happened due to the efforts of two British communists, Philip Spratt and Benjamin Bradley. With financial support from Moscow, Spratt managed to organize

---

[8] *Selected Works of M.N. Roy Volume I: 1917-1922*, edited by Sibnarayan Ray, Oxford University Press, 1987.

a small number of units before the British arrested several of the activists in 1929. In what is known as the Meerut Conspiracy Case, the accused were defended by no less than Jawaharlal Nehru and K.N. Katju. The trial went on until 1933 and twenty-seven persons were given sentences of various lengths. More importantly, it provided a great deal of publicity to the communists and created interest in their ideas. Similarly, Roy's colourful life also attracted a lot of admirers.

There is a fair amount of first-hand evidence that the British deliberately encouraged the spread of Marxist literature among political prisoners in the early 1930s. It is likely that the British had infiltrated the Indian communist movement and felt that they could misdirect its energies. This was entirely in character with colonial tactics.

M.N. Roy, meanwhile, had appealed against his sentence and managed to reduce the prison term to six years. He was

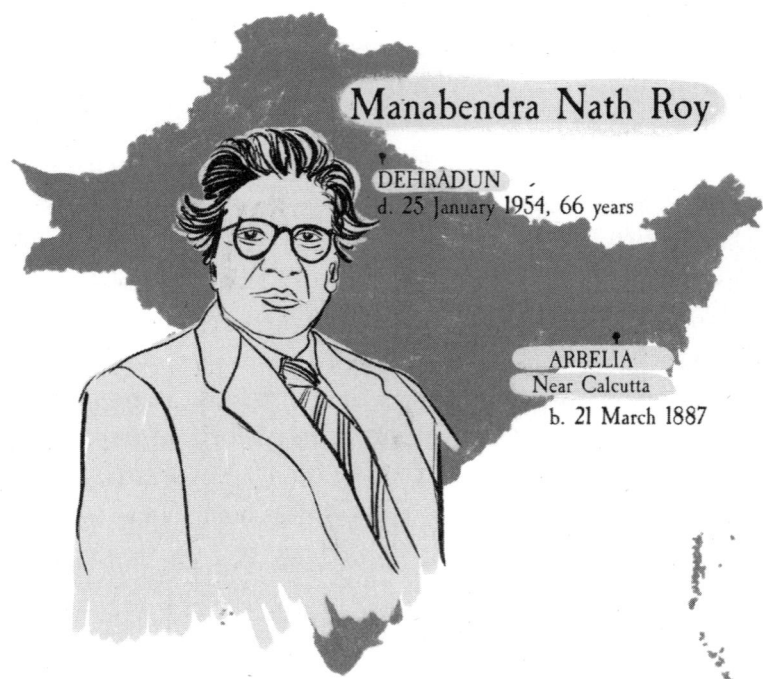

Manabendra Nath Roy

DEHRADUN
d. 25 January 1954, 66 years

ARBELIA
Near Calcutta
b. 21 March 1887

released in November 1936 and joined the Congress. With Nehru's help, he was even elected to the All India Congress Committee.[9] Roy's commitment to the communist cause was now wavering. Not only was he uncomfortable with foreign influences in the CPI, he was beginning to question several Marxist ideas. Eventually, he drifted off to develop his own complex ideology and became largely irrelevant by the 1940s.

The Founding of the RSS

Keshav Baliram Hedgewar was born into a family of modest means in Nagpur in 1889. He lost both his parents to an epidemic when he was just thirteen. Thereafter, he was supported by family members and a charismatic local leader, Dr B.S. Moonje. When he was in high school, Hedgewar was deeply influenced by the nationalist ideas being spread by Tilak and became the leader of a band of students. When the inspector of schools visited, he arranged for the whole class to shout 'Vande Mataram' when the official entered the room. The principal attempted to find out who was behind this but failed. Thus, the whole class was suspended. The news spread and it led to students in several Nagpur schools boycotting class. The authorities eventually accepted back most of Hedgewar's classmates on the basis of a written apology, but he adamantly refused to write one. Thus, young Keshav Baliram ended up being expelled.[10]

Hedgewar was now forced to move to Pune for his studies and then, with the blessings of Dr Moonje, to Calcutta to pursue a medical degree at National Medical College in 1910. This was one of several nationalist institutions that had been recently set up to bypass the control of the British on the education system.

[9] *Ibid.*
[10] Nilanjan Mukhopadhyay, *The RSS: Icons of the Indian Right*, Tranquebar, 2019.

Given his political leanings, it is not surprising that Hedgewar was soon initiated into the Anushilan Samiti. Evidently, he even learnt to speak Bengali and dress like a local. He was given the code name 'Cocaine' and assigned the job of delivering messages, pamphlets and revolvers to different units. By 1913, he had earned himself a licentiate in medicine and surgery—although this degree was not yet recognized formally by the colonial administration as it was issued by a 'native' institution. The newly minted doctor moved back to Nagpur with instructions to set up an Anushilan Samiti unit there. He quickly reconnected with his old friends and set up an organization named Kranti Dal (Revolutionary Party).

Like most other revolutionaries, Hedgewar saw the First World War as an opportunity to strike against the British Empire. The Kranti Dal attempted to smuggle in German small arms through the Portuguese enclave of Goa. Unfortunately, the attempt was foiled when the British seized the ship at sea. Deprived of an adequate supply of arms, Hedgewar and his group decided to throw in their lot with Tilak, who had returned from Mandalay and started to re-energize the Congress.

The INC session was held in Nagpur in 1920. As a local trusted by Tilak, Hedgewar was involved in raising a volunteer force of over a thousand to manage the event. It was to be Tilak's moment, but he passed away a few months before the session. The event, instead, saw the launch of Gandhi's Non-Cooperation Movement. Again, like most revolutionaries, Hedgewar was not entirely convinced either by the insistence on strict non-violence or by the mobilization of Muslims using a communal cause such as Khilafat. Nonetheless, he seems to have participated with enthusiasm and, in 1921, was arrested and charged with sedition. He decided to plead his own case, so that he could make a bold statement on India belonging to Indians.

Hedgewar was found guilty and sentenced to a year in prison. By the time he was released, Gandhi had withdrawn the movement. Although he returned to a hero's welcome in Nagpur, he was deeply disillusioned, just like many other revolutionaries. Hedgewar decided to set up an organization that could weld together the Hindu community (defined broadly to include Buddhists, Jains and Sikhs). The RSS was founded on Vijaya Dashami in September 1925.

The RSS was soon establishing branches (called *shakhas*) across the country. The organizational structure was likely influenced by the idea of a network of akhadas, as had been envisaged by the original Anushilan Samiti. Importantly, the organization was designed strictly as a sociocultural body that would keep away from active politics. Hedgewar was clear that members were welcome, even encouraged, to participate in the freedom movement but the RSS as an organization would not participate in anything political.

The adamant refusal to let the RSS get involved directly in politics displeased many of his potential allies. Vinayak Savarkar, finally fully freed in 1937, had decided to take up the Hindu cause and was trying to expand the Hindu Mahasabha as a political party to represent the community. He appears to have been both puzzled and annoyed by the RSS's insistence on staying away from politics.

By the time Hedgewar passed away in June 1940, the RSS had grown beyond its Maharashtra heartland and established *shakhas* across the subcontinent—Lahore, Karachi, Delhi,

Rawalpindi, Calcutta, Madras and so on. It had an estimated 60,000 members by this time and was attracting the attention of British intelligence.

The Rebel President

After the Hijli incident, Subhas Bose had been touring the country. It was quite clear that he had inherited the legacy of C.R. Das and Tilak. Combined with his links to the revolutionaries, he was emerging as the most important national-level leader after Gandhi. In December 1931, he travelled to Maharashtra, where he presided over the Maharashtra Youth Conference held at the Shivaji Mandir in Pune. He then travelled to Satara, Karad and Sholapur, where he was met by large crowds.[11]

Following his unsuccessful negotiations in London, Gandhi returned to India on 28 December. The public mood was charged with disappointment and Viceroy Willingdon saw Subhas as fanning the flames. On 3 January 1932, he was arrested at Kalyan on his way back to Calcutta. A day later, Gandhi and other senior leaders of the INC were also arrested.

Yet again, Subhas fell seriously ill in prison. It was only in mid-January 1933 that the government agreed to let Bose travel to Europe for treatment. He was given a passport that was only valid for France and Switzerland (although it was later extended to other countries). Bose sailed out from Bombay on 23 February on *SS Gange*.

> While undergoing treatment at Clinique La Lignière in Geneva, Switzerland, Bose spent a lot of time with Vithalbhai Patel, the elder brother of Vallabhbhai, who was

[11] Chandrachur Ghose, *Bose: The Untold Story of an Inconvenient Nationalist*, Penguin Random House India, 2022.

also undergoing treatment there. Vithalbhai was the last of the senior Swarajist leaders, and his views were more closely aligned with Bose's rather than Gandhi's. The two grew close and Subhas diligently attended to the older man in his last days. After his death, it emerged that Vithalbhai had bequeathed a significant portion of his assets, valued at that time at Rs 1 lakh, to Subhas.[12] This would lead to an ugly legal dispute with the Patel family.

Although Bose was away from India, he was constantly thinking about developments back home. By mid-1934, the non-violent branch of the freedom movement had also got stuck in a quagmire. It was then in Vienna that Bose began to write *The Indian Struggle*, where he provided a first-hand account of events in the country. He hired a young Austrian woman, Emilie Schenkl, who knew English, to help him type and edit the book. The two would fall in love and, years later, get married.

This was a time of intense ideological turmoil in the world and Bose witnessed a Europe caught up in it. Two ideologies—fascism and communism—were on the rise and everyone was expected to take sides. From his various speeches and writings, one can see that Bose was essentially a pragmatist, who did not want ideology to divert him from his main mission of freeing India from foreign domination.

Bose landed in Bombay on 8 April 1936. He was arrested on the docks and taken away to Arthur Road Prison. He was later kept under house arrest at his brother's house in Kurseong, in northern Bengal. The countrywide provincial elections held in early 1937 went well for the INC with a clear majority in six out of eleven provinces, and in a position to

[12] *Ibid.*

form a government in two more. This was the situation when Subhas Bose was released from house arrest in March 1937.

In mid-January 1938, Subhas Bose was informed that Gandhi had chosen him as the next president of the INC. The Haripura Congress held in February 1938 was quite a grand affair. One of the issues that Subhas championed as president was the proper treatment and early release of political prisoners. Many of these prisoners were from the revolutionary movement.

It was probably in this context that he met Sachin Sanyal, who had recently returned from his second stint in Cellular Jail. They met in October on the sidelines of the Durga Puja celebrations on Lucknow's Hewitt Road, the city's oldest puja. Sanyal was living in the area with relatives and yet again trying to re-establish his network. We know from surviving letters that Sanyal had already re-established contact with his old comrade Rashbehari Bose in Japan. We do not know exactly what Subhas and Sanyal discussed, but it is likely that they discussed the gathering clouds of war and the possibilities it presented. A few days later, they visited Lucknow District Jail to meet the political prisoners lodged there.

It was also around this time that Subhas Bose made up his mind to seek a second term as INC president. There was significant support for this among the rank and file of the party, and several prominent individuals such as Rabindranath Tagore were in favour of it. In contrast, Gandhi and his loyalists were adamantly against this. They wanted Maulana Abul Kalam Azad as the next president. Hectic meetings took place within the Gandhian camp in December as it became obvious that Bose was not going to back down from a contest. Eventually, Abul Kalam announced on 20 January 1939 that he was stepping aside for Pattabhi Sitaramayya, a staunch Gandhi loyalist from Andhra Pradesh. A few days later, the Gandhian group—Vallabhbhai Patel, Rajendra Prasad, Jairamdas Doulatram, J.B. Kripalani, Jamnalal Bajaj and others—wrote to Subhas Bose to step down in favour of Sitaramayya. Bose refused. There was no escaping an electoral contest.

Bose's confidence drew from a broad pool of support that included the youth, various Left-leaning groups, former revolutionaries, the remnants of C.R. Das's Swarajists and so on. Most Left-leaning groups, meanwhile, had coalesced around the newly created Congress Socialist Party (CSP), which functioned as a loose bloc within the INC. The CSP also had the support of the communists. Thus, Bose had the direct or indirect support of a strong coalition.

Despite their internal differences, the revolutionaries threw themselves into drumming up support for Subhas Bose. When the ballots were counted, Bose beat Sitaramayya 1,580 to 1,377 delegates. The revolutionary strongholds of Bengal, Punjab and United Provinces had voted overwhelmingly for Bose.

Despite the clear election defeat, the Gandhi loyalists were not willing to cede control or cooperate. Twelve members of the Working Committee resigned. Bose was especially hurt that it included Jawaharlal Nehru, who he had felt would be an ally against the old guard. The Tripuri Congress in March, therefore, began in an atmosphere of intrigue. What made it worse for Subhas was that he was very unwell and had to be carried to the venue on a stretcher.

Subhas had hoped that he would be able to get his way as he had, after all, won the election comfortably. However, following a heated debate over the nomination of the Working Committee, the CSP convener Jayaprakash Narayan decided suddenly to turn 'neutral'. Without support from the CSP, Bose's position was suddenly weak. He again reached out to Nehru but it only resulted in a caustic exchange of letters. With no room to manoeuvre, Subhas was forced to resign, and Rajendra Prasad succeeded him. As soon as Prasad became president, he nominated Dr Bidhan Chandra Roy and Prafulla Chandra Ghosh, both from the Gandhian faction, as the Bengali representatives in the Working Committee.

From here on, nothing that Subhas did in the political sphere seemed to go right. He decided to unite the various Left-leaning groups within the INC under the umbrella of a new group called Forward Bloc. He held meetings with the Anushilan Marxists, the Royists and the CSP to elicit their support but received a mixed response. Subhas Bose's increasing emphasis on the Left, meanwhile, alienated his non-Left supporters such as the Jugantar nationalists. They had been fellow travellers from the C.R. Das era and felt that they were being taken for granted.

Under the influence of his elder brother Sarat, Subhas also began to get deeply involved in the politics of the Calcutta Municipal Corporation. This was a mistake, as it merely diminished his stature from that of a national-level leader to that of a local politician. With the Forward Bloc and Gandhian factions of the Bengal Congress not on speaking terms, Dr Nalinaksha Sanyal emerged as the Chief Whip of the INC in the provincial assembly. He was associated with the Jugantar nationalists but had good personal relations with the Bose brothers and Dr B.C. Roy.

Preparing for a Second Ghadar

Subhas Bose had begun 1939 in triumph but ended the year in shambles. The escalating war in Europe, however, changed the political dynamics yet again. Here was another opportunity to ignite an armed rebellion in India. Subhas always had a soft corner for the revolutionaries, but now he decided to join them.

After returning from prison in 1937, Sachindra Nath Sanyal had been gradually re-establishing his network across India as well as re-connecting with remnants of the international Ghadarite network through Rashbehari Bose. This was not easy, since he was constantly under surveillance. With train stations under constant watch, he would send his cousins to ride long distances on horseback to deliver secret messages! Interestingly, Sanyal was in touch with the Japanese consul well before the war. His son would later recount how he had been witness to late-night meetings between his father, Subhas Bose and Japanese officials in 1939–40.

Sachin Sanyal's writings from this period suggest that he still retained his distrust of Marxism, and was distressed about how ideological differences had divided the movement in his absence (even his brother Bhupendra had become a Royist). Nonetheless, the smell of a possible armed rebellion attracted some of the former revolutionaries back to the fold. The Anushilan Marxists, who had drifted away from nationalist revolutionaries on grounds of ideology, now drifted back.

Using the reconstituted revolutionary network, Subhas Bose and Sanyal reached out to a large number of old revolutionary leaders. Feelers were sent out to Akbar Shah in the North West Frontier, Bhai Parmanand in Lahore, Keshab Hedgewar in Nagpur, Ganesh Savarkar and so on.[13] The revolutionaries were heartened by the overall response. Interestingly, Jogesh Chandra Chatterjee mentions in his biography that the famously apolitical Hedgewar went as far as to offer the 44,000-strong RSS cadre if an armed insurrection could be triggered during the war.[14] The revolutionary fervour of the former Anushilan Samiti activist was still alive, but he passed away in June 1940.

Unfortunately, British intelligence was also aware that something was cooking.

Intelligence officials soon found out that Subhas had met soldiers of 1/15 Punjab Regiment several times in 1939 with the help of Niranjan Singh Talib. They also discovered that Trailokyanath Chakraborty, a well-known Anushilan Samiti operative, was in the Chittagong hill tracts collecting arms and building a network. At that time, the British colonial administration was desperately galvanizing resources in India to help the war effort, and these discoveries came as a shock. Four soldiers from the Punjab Regiment were arrested. So was Chakraborty. The revolutionaries had primed Naik Indar Singh, the key contact in the regiment, to raise the national flag in Calcutta's Fort William as a sign of revolt. Sensing that something was afoot, the authorities moved the regiment out of Calcutta, and the plan was never carried out.[15]

For Sachin Sanyal, all of this would have felt like déjà vu. They had come so close to an 1857-style revolt in 1915 but failed. The effort in 1939–40 seemed to be unravelling at an even earlier stage. Unknown to him, however, a lone HSRA operative in London was about to carry out a major strike.

---

[13] Nimaichand Pramanik, *Gandhi and the Revolutionaries*, University of Calcutta, 1982.
[14] Jogesh Chandra Chatterjee, *In Search of Freedom*, published by Paresh Chandra Chatterjee, 1958 (printed by B.K. Majumdar, Calcutta).
[15] Chandrachur Ghose, *Bose: The Untold Story of an Inconvenient Nationalist*, Penguin Random House India, 2022.

Avenging Jallianwala

Udham Singh was born in December 1899 as Sher Singh in the home of a poor peasant in Sunam, Patiala State (today in Sangrur district of Punjab). His mother died when he was three and his father when he was five years old. He and his brother were admitted into an orphanage in Amritsar run by the Chief Khalsa Diwan. It was here that the boy was rebaptized and given the name Ude Singh.[16]

Ude Singh's brother died of pneumonia in 1913. At the age of seventeen, Ude briefly joined the British Indian Army and was sent to Basra. Although it was only a brief stint, it gave him a taste for travel that he retained for the rest of his life.

Ude was back in the orphanage in Amritsar by the end of 1918, and was in the city when the Jallianwala massacre took place on 13 April 1919. Some accounts suggest that he may have actually seen the shooting, but it is more likely he heard the shots and visited the site a couple of hours later. The scene that he witnessed had a profound impact on the young man. Ude and some others from the orphanage tried to help the victims as best they could, but given the lockdown, there was little they could do other than provide drinking water and help relatives carry the dead and dying.

Like many others, Ude was outraged when several leading Punjabis came out in support of the British after the massacre. It is said that Ude went a few days later to the Golden Temple and swore while taking a dip in the holy tank that he would avenge the massacre.[17] It would take him two decades.

Over the next couple of months, Ude came under the influence of Lala Lajpat Rai. He attended political meetings and avidly read nationalist literature. It was during this time

---

[16] Sikandar Singh, *Udham Singh: A Saga of the Freedom Movement and Jallianwala Bagh*, B. Chattar Singh Jiwan Singh, Amritsar, 2017 edition.
[17] *Ibid.*

that he met his hero Bhagat Singh, who was then at National College, Lahore. As a trained carpenter, Ude got a job with the Uganda Railway Workshops and left for Africa. Using his earnings from working there for two years, Ude travelled to Mexico, the United States and Europe. While in California, he connected with the Ghadarites and witnessed veteran revolutionary Mahendra Pratap deliver a fiery speech at the gurudwara in Stockton in early 1924.

After living and working in many other places, Ude Singh returned to India in July 1927. It seems by the time he reached Amritsar a few weeks later, police intelligence had marked him out as a potential Ghadarite. He was arrested in late August and charged for the possession of two revolvers and an automatic pistol. He had purchased them in the United States but did not have a gun licence for India. He was sentenced as Sher Singh, his birth name, to five years of rigorous imprisonment. He was still in jail when he heard of the hanging of Bhagat Singh. It served as a reminder of his own oath.

On being released from jail, he applied for a passport under the name Udham Singh in March 1933. After extensive travels, Udham Singh ended up in Coventry, England. He seems to have taken up many different jobs to earn a living. By mid-1939, he shifted to London, where he frequented the gurudwara at 79 Sinclair Road, Shepherd's Bush. His occasional nationalist statements, however, made the gurudwara management wary of him. Over the previous few years, the British authorities had systematically replaced Ghadarites in gurudwara management committees with Loyalists from across the empire. They were uncomfortable with people such as Udham Singh, who expressed revolutionary sentiments.

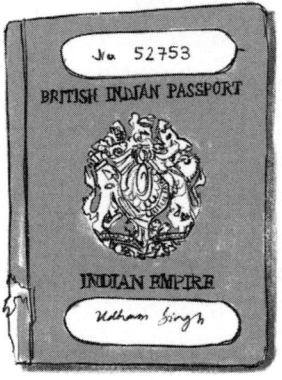

There is reason to believe that Udham had originally planned to kill Reginald Dyer, but Dyer had died several years earlier. Therefore, he turned his attention to Sir Michael O'Dwyer, who had been the lieutenant governor of Punjab at the time of the Jallianwala massacre. His notes later showed that he was aware of where O'Dwyer lived but had decided against assassinating him at home. This was to be a political act done in full public view.

Udham eventually decided on an event organized by the Royal Central Asian Society at Caxton Hall on 13 March 1940. This was the same venue where Vinayak Savarkar had stood up to defend Madanlal Dhingra's actions three decades earlier. As a bonus, Lord Zetland, secretary of state for India, was also going to be present at the event.

The meeting started at 3 p.m. The hall was packed with around four hundred people. No one paid attention to a well-dressed Indian in a blue pin-striped suit and red tie.[18] The event had just ended when Udham Singh pulled out a revolver and fired six bullets in quick succession. The first two shots were aimed at O'Dwyer, who died almost instantly with a bullet through his heart. The next two were aimed at Zetland, who fell from his chair but was only mildly grazed. The next shot went through the arm of Sir Louis Dane while the last shot shattered Lord Lamington's right hand.

At this point, Udham Singh's revolver was out of ammunition. He had more bullets in his pocket but did not have time to reload as several members of the audience jumped on him. When the police handcuffed him a few minutes later and took him away, Udham Singh was photographed smiling. He had finally avenged Jallianwala.

When the Scotland Yard interrogators asked Udham his name, he replied, 'Ram Mohammed Singh Azad'. This mixed name is significant in the context of communal tensions back in India and the growing demands for Pakistan. Of course, further investigations soon revealed his real identity.

Udham Singh was initially sent to Brixton Prison and then shifted to Pentonville. He was hanged at Pentonville on 30 July 1940 from the same gallows as Madanlal Dhingra. These two men from Amritsar, separated by a generation, gave their lives at the same spot for the same dream of a free India.

> Udham Singh's remains were brought back to India in July 1974 and received a hero's welcome. The *kalash* with his ashes is kept on display at the Jallianwala Bagh museum in Amritsar.

[18] *Ibid.*

◆ 8 ◆
'ONE MORE FIGHT. THE LAST AND THE BEST'

GERMANY INVADED POLAND in September 1939, and Britain and France soon entered the war. By April 1940, the Nazis had taken over Denmark and Norway, and were bearing down on Belgium and Holland. By late May, the British Expeditionary Force was trapped in Dunkirk and had to be evacuated in a desperate effort. On 14 June, the Germans entered Paris without opposition.

This rapid sequence of events was watched closely by all political groups in India. The general pre-war feeling in the Congress was that India should not be dragged into another war: *'India cannot fight for freedom unless she herself was free.'*[1] Nevertheless, when Britain declared war in September 1939, Viceroy Linlithgow unilaterally issued a proclamation that India was a party to the war against Germany.

Even as Gandhi vacillated, two views emerged in the INC. On one side was Nehru, who was for India to stand with Britain. The alternative view was that of Subhas Bose, who remained adamant that India should keep out of the war and focus on liberating itself from foreign occupation. The Congress leadership soon realized that the general mood swayed towards the latter. A party resolution on 10 October states: *'India must be declared an independent nation, and present application must be given to this status to the largest possible extent.'*[2]

Faced with such intransigence on one hand and a rapidly deteriorating military position on the other, the viceroy made the 'August Offer' on 8 August 1940, which promised to set up a body to frame a new constitution after the war. At the

---
[1] *Struggle for Freedom*, edited by R.C. Majumdar, Bharatiya Vidya Bhavan, 1969 (reprinted in 1979).
[2] *Ibid.*

same time, it used language that seemed to provide a veto to the Muslim League in the name of protecting minority rights. The colonial authorities then played for time by stoking the League's growing demands for a Partition of India along religious lines.

Former and active members of the revolutionary movement had a variety of views on the evolving situation and India's participation in the war. Vinayak Savarkar, now leader of the Hindu Mahasabha, was of the view that Hindus should enthusiastically enlist in the army. Savarkar believed that the British would be too weak to hold India after the war and would inevitably leave. His concern was that if they left behind an Indian army that was dominated by Muslims, it would result in yet another Islamic conquest of India. This was not an idle concern in the context of the increasingly shrill demands for Partition and growing communal tensions. Thus, Savarkar wanted to make sure that there was an adequate number of well-trained Hindu/Sikh regiments available for post-Independence exigencies. He would be proved right when India and Pakistan would go to war over Jammu and Kashmir within months of gaining freedom.

The Anushilan Marxists, led by Jogesh Chandra Chatterjee,[3] had formed a new party called the Revolutionary Socialist Party of India in 1940. They remained opposed to the British throughout the war. The CPI was initially unsure of its position, but by mid-1941, enthusiastically collaborated with the British authorities.

The revolutionary network, being revived by Sachin Sanyal and Rashbehari Bose, had remained committed to the old idea of fomenting a revolt in the British Indian armed forces. They saw the Second World War as a chance to

---

[3] Jogesh Chandra Chatterjee, *In Search of Freedom*, published by Paresh Chandra Chatterjee, 1958 (printed by B.K. Majumdar, Calcutta).

complete what they had started in the previous war. Despite their discomfort with Nazism and Japanese imperialism, they were focused on ending the British occupation of their motherland. Similarly, they were willing to work with the Anushilan Marxists despite their differing viewpoints.

As we have seen in the previous chapter, the intelligence agencies were aware of the active revolutionaries and keeping a close watch. When they found out that Sanyal had met the Japanese envoy in Varanasi in 1940, he was arrested once again and sent to Deoli Detention Camp. In a deliberate act, the British put him in a cramped cell with a dying tuberculosis patient. Sanyal nursed the man until his last breath but himself contracted the disease, which was considered incurable at that time. Repeated appeals for his release were rejected, even as his health deteriorated sharply.[4] When it was clear that he would not survive, his relatives were allowed to take him away. He died a few days later in Gorakhpur on 6 February 1942. A patriot who had inspired, recruited and organized several generations of revolutionaries was no more.

The Escape

Subhas Bose was arrested again on 2 July 1940. The Battle of Britain was raging and the outcome was far from certain. The colonial authorities were not taking chances with a man who could sway a large segment of the population. In November, Subhas swore on the Goddess Kali that he would fast unto death unless he was released. The viceroy soon realized that this was no empty threat; the last thing he needed was a leader of Subhas' stature dying in custody. He was released on 5 December and allowed to go home to Calcutta.

---

[4] 'Reminiscences of Shri J.N. Mukherjee, J.N. Sanyal and Others', Commemorative brochure for the 90th year of Sachindra Nath Sanyal, 1983.

A frail Subhas was lodged in his late father's bedroom at 38/2 Elgin Road. The large, airy room had a four-poster bed, a smaller cot, a painting of Goddess Kali, a tiger-skin rug for meditation, a low table with books (including the Bhagawad Gita) and some family photographs. Several members of the extended family occupied rooms in the rest of the house. Outside the house, the government had deployed a large number of policemen in plain clothes to keep watch, and all his correspondence was intercepted and monitored by the post office.

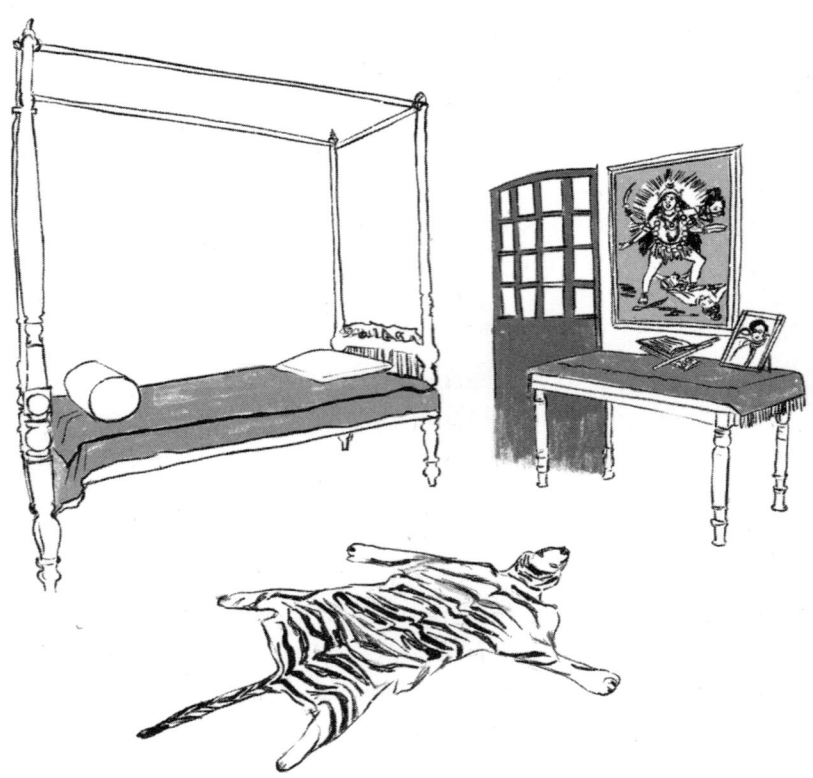

Subhas had no intention of spending the war stuck in limbo. The fluid geopolitical situation provided an opportunity that was too good to be wasted, but he knew he would be arrested if he did anything within India. He needed to find a way to get out of the country. So, he approached his nephew, Sisir.

In mid-December, the Forward Bloc's provincial head for the North West Frontier Province, Akbar Shah, visited Calcutta. Sisir accompanied him to Wachel Molla's department store and purchased some baggy salwar trousers and a black fez cap. He also purchased a suitcase, toiletries, a bed roll and so on. Finally, he went to a printing shop and ordered visiting cards that read: 'Mohd. Ziauddin, B.A., LL.B., Travelling Inspector, The Empire of India Life Assurance Co. Ltd., Permanent Address: Civil Lines, Jubblepore.'[5]

From his window, Subhas could see the policemen assigned to keep watch. During the day, they walked around, but at night they huddled in blankets around a charpoy at the crossing of Elgin Road and Woodburn Park Road.

By 16 January 1941, Subhas was ready to execute his plan. He announced to his family and friends that he was going into religious seclusion for a while, as he wanted to spend time meditating. At 1.35 a.m. the plan was put into motion. Subhas transformed into Mohammad Ziauddin, dressed in a long coat, a baggy salwar and a black fez. Sisir and another nephew quietly carried his luggage to Sisir's car. The car went out of the gate, took a right and then another right into a narrow lane named Allenby Road to avoid the policemen at the crossing further ahead. Sisir next took a left on to Lansdowne Road before he breathed a sigh of relief. They had escaped the immediate cordon.

[5] Sugata Bose, *His Majesty's Opponent*, Penguin India, 2013.

The duo travelled unimpeded until they reached the home of a relative near Dhanbad by 8.30 a.m. After a brief period of rest, Subhas was dropped off at Gomoh railway station, where he boarded the *Delhi–Kalka Mail*. Still disguised as Ziauddin, he next boarded the *Frontier Mail* from Delhi to Peshawar, where he was greeted by Akbar Shah on 19 January. He was taken to the Taj Mahal Hotel. The staff must have been impressed by their scholarly and devout guest, for they provided him a room with a prayer rug!

The next stage of the journey into Afghanistan needed a new disguise. Subhas now transformed into a deaf and mute Pathan going on a pilgrimage to the shrine of Adda Sharif. He was accompanied by Bhagat Ram Talwar, a local communist, disguised as a relative named Rahmat Khan.[6]

Meanwhile, back in Calcutta, the police and most of the Bose household continued to be oblivious to the escape. Food was dutifully taken into the seclusion room but was eaten by the two nephews and a niece. It was only on 26 January that the disappearance was discovered by the cooks, who raised an alarm. The viceroy was furious when he heard the news and the press reports turned the Bengal provincial authorities into a laughing stock. By this time, Subhas and Bhagat Ram had crossed into Afghanistan.

The two arrived in Kabul on 31 January. Bose knew that he could not linger in the city for too long, as there were many British agents around. If they identified him, it would not be difficult to bribe a few tribesmen to kidnap him and bundle him back into British-controlled territory. Thus, after a few days in hiding, he decided to barge into the German embassy. The German officials cabled Berlin for instructions.

While he waited for a reply, Bose also contacted the Italian embassy. Pietro Quaroni, the Italian minister in Kabul,

[6] *Ibid.*

arranged for an Italian passport for Bose under the name Orlando Mazzotta, a diplomatic courier. The Italian, German and Soviet diplomats then worked out an escape route. Subhas made his way on foot through the Hindukush passes to the Soviet frontier on the Oxus river, where he was picked up and driven to Samarkand. From there he went by train to Moscow and reported at the Italian embassy. He eventually flew to Berlin on 2 April 1941.

Quit India

From the very beginning of the war, Prime Minister Winston Churchill had been trying to coax a reluctant President Roosevelt to join the war on the side of the Allies. Eventually, Britain and the United States issued the Atlantic Charter in August 1941, which declared that: *'They respect the right of all people to choose the form of Government under which they will live; and they wish to see sovereign rights and self-Government restored to those who have been forcibly deprived of them.'*[7] However, Churchill clarified a few weeks later in the House of Commons that the Atlantic Charter did not apply to India. This was blatant hypocrisy and caused a breakdown of trust.

The war took a sharp turn after Japan entered in December 1941 by simultaneously attacking Pearl Harbor and the Malay peninsula. By 15 February, they had taken Singapore, hitherto considered an impregnable fortress. This naturally weakened Britain's position in India and the War Cabinet realized that some concrete promises had to be made. In March 1942, Sir Stafford Cripps was sent to India to discuss the terms of a draft declaration. The draft accepted that self-government would be introduced as soon as possible and that a constitution-

---

[7] As quoted in *Struggle for Freedom*, edited by R.C. Majumdar, Bharatiya Vidya Bhavan, 1969 (reprinted in 1979).

making body would be set up 'immediately upon cessation of hostilities'. This was a big step forward.

The declaration, however, also included a provision that provinces and princely states that did not want to join the Indian Union were free to frame their own constitution. This was included as a way to assuage the Muslim League and the various Indian princes, but INC leaders saw it as a cynical move to facilitate Partition as well as to encourage the princely states to chart an independent course. The breakdown of trust was complete.

At this time, the old revolutionary Aurobindo Ghosh reappeared on the political stage after being absent for three decades. During these years, he had turned into Sri Aurobindo, a much-revered spiritual guru in French-ruled Pondicherry, and his earlier career as a freedom fighter was just a faint memory. Thus, everyone was taken aback by his sudden political intervention.

In an open letter, Sri Aurobindo welcomed the Cripps Mission and urged the political class to take it seriously. He then sent Duraiswami Iyer as a special emissary to the Congress Working Committee, urging the members to take up the proposals. He felt that India needed to stand with the Allies against Nazism and that the Cripps proposals provided a definite path towards freedom as well as towards a framework for discussion with various parties on how to keep India united.[8]

Some Congress leaders did share Sri Aurobindo's views. C. Rajagopalachari even managed to pass a resolution in the Madras legislature that broadly supported the Cripps approach. However, Gandhi and INC president Abul Kalam expressed their disapproval, and Rajagopalachari was forced

---

[8] *Sri Aurobindo and the Cripps Mission*, edited by Sunayana Panda, Sri Aurobindo Ashram Press, 2012.

to resign. In a broadcast on the All India Radio on 11 April 1942, Stafford Cripps publicly withdrew the proposals.

With the failure of the Cripps Mission, the stage was set for Gandhi to launch a new round of civil disobedience. On 12 July, the Congress Working Committee passed a resolution that is commonly referred to as the 'Quit India' proclamation. It demanded that British rule in India end with immediate effect. The political establishment in London was not pleased. Within weeks, Gandhi and most INC leaders were arrested and the party's headquarters in Allahabad sealed.

Despite the lack of any senior leadership, the Quit India Movement spread quickly across the country. Large protests spontaneously took place, there were many industrial strikes and widespread arson caused damage to public property. In many campuses, such as Banaras Hindu University, the students created 'liberated zones', where they took over the administration and issued their own entry passes. The government responded with full-scale repression. The military machinery was already mobilized in anticipation of a Japanese invasion and its fury was directed at the civilian

population. Some 60,000 people were arrested and thousands were shot dead. No one knows for sure how many protesters were killed, but the number was likely higher than 10,000 and perhaps as high as 25,000. Leaderless and faced with such vicious repression, the Quit India Movement was crushed by early 1943.

The Indian Independence League

Rashbehari Bose had arrived in Japan in 1915 and lived in the country ever since. He had not been able to visit India in all these years as he was still considered dangerous and would have been immediately arrested. Nonetheless, he had remained committed to the struggle for Independence and had closely followed events in India. He continued to write prolifically, a lot of it in Japanese. He was a well-respected member of the expatriate Indian community in Tokyo and regularly hosted prominent Indian visitors.

He also kept up correspondence with many Indian leaders, including those of the INC. At the same time, he also advised leaders from other colonized Asian countries on their freedom struggles. In the age of stormy ideological battles, Rashbehari remained committed to an earlier era of nationalism, to Pan-Asianism and to the Hindu ideals of Dharma. With support from the Japanese establishment, Rashbehari edited and published a dual language Pan-Asianist journal named *The New Asia – Shin Ajia*, which was soon banned in British India but found widespread underground circulation in Southeast Asia.[9]

[9] Cemil Aydin, *Japan's Pan-Asianism and the Legitimacy of Imperial World Order, 1931-1945*, The Asia-Pacific Journal, Vol 6, Issue 3, 3 March 2008.

In the late 1930s, Rashbehari was able to re-establish contact with his old comrade, Sachindra Nath Sanyal, who had returned after a decade in the Cellular Jail. Their letters suggest that they retained their friendship and mutual respect, despite the decades of separation.[10] Similarly, we know that Subhas was in touch with the older Bose in the late 1930s. The latter wrote admiringly about Subhas in Japanese publications.

Rashbehari was also in touch with other Indian nationalists based in east Asia. There was a particularly active group in Bangkok led by Giani Pritam Singh and Swami Satyananda Puri. Together they formed the Indian Independence League (IIL). Their efforts got a boost from Japanese gains in Southeast Asia during the early phase of the war. In March 1942, Rashbehari organized a conference in Tokyo for this group. It was here that a resolution was passed to form the Indian National Army (INA), or the Azad Hind Fauj, using recruits from Indian expatriates and surrendered soldiers of British Indian forces. Unfortunately, Pritam Singh and Satyananda Puri died in a plane crash on their way to Tokyo, and Rashbehari was suddenly deprived of two trusted comrades.

A second conference was held in June, with delegates from Malaya, Hong Kong, Singapore, Indonesia, Thailand, Indo-China and so on. The tricolour was flown and a formal constitution was drawn up, stating that the IIL's objective was the complete independence of India.

The question arose of finding a suitable commander for the INA. None of the revolutionary leaders had any formal military training. Pritam Singh and Iwaichi Fujiwara, a Japanese officer, had earlier decided on Captain Mohan Singh of the 1/14 Punjab Regiment, who had surrendered to the Japanese during the early phase of the invasion of north

---

[10] The Sanyal family has loaned most of the letters to the Biplobi Bharat Museum at Victoria Memorial, Kolkata, and to the Nehru Memorial Library, Delhi.

Malaya in December 1941. The Bangkok conference in June 1942 elected Rashbehari Bose as the president. He was to be assisted by a four-member council. Mohan Singh was made a member of the council in his capacity as commander-in-chief.

Bose made an appeal over radio broadcasts for volunteers to join an army of liberation. After the fall of Singapore, the Indian prisoners of war were separated from the others and brought to Farrer Park. Here, Japanese officials, translated by Colonel N.S. Gill, gave them the choice of joining the INA. By the end of August 1942, around 40,000 prisoners of war had signed up for the new army. They were joined by many expatriate Indians, mostly Tamil, living in Singapore and Malaya.

With the support of the Japanese, arrangements were made for the housing and training of INA soldiers. However, after the initial momentum, internal divisions and power struggles arose. Unfortunately, at this critical juncture, Rashbehari's health deteriorated sharply. His diabetes became worse and he contracted pulmonary tuberculosis. He was ageing, suffering from poor health and yet so close to achieving what he had attempted all his life. One finds the following line written on many of his personal notes from this time, as if he was willing himself on: 'I was a fighter. One more fight, the last and the best.'[11]

Chalo Dilli

Subhas Bose arrived in Berlin as Orlando Mazzotta on 2 April 1941, and was given a quasi-diplomatic status. He immediately put together a detailed plan on how the Germans could undermine the British by fomenting a

---

[11] Takeshi Nakajima, *Bose of Nakamuraya: An Indian Revolutionary in Japan*, translated from Japanese by Prem Motwani, Promilla & Co, 2005.

revolution in India and the Middle East. Importantly, he argued that this needed a clear statement from the Germans on Indian Independence.

Subhas had hoped for two things when arrived in Berlin. First, an early meeting with Hitler to pitch his ideas directly to the top German leadership. Second, a clear declaration of support for the Indian freedom movement. He would be disappointed on both accounts. Bose decided to head for Rome. It was here that he heard that Germany had invaded the Soviet Union. This came as a shock to him. In his characteristically frank style, he made it clear to the Germans that he thought this was a terrible mistake.

The German attack on the Soviet Union also compromised Subhas's direct communications link with his supporters in India. Bhagat Ram Talwar, who had helped Subhas reach Kabul, now switched sides. Instead of carrying Bose's messages to the intended recipients, Talwar now reported them to British intelligence and to his communist handlers. In turn, they wrote misleading replies that were passed back to Bose through the Axis embassies in Kabul.[12]

Subhas returned to Berlin in the third week of July and, by October, was able to establish the office of the Free India Centre at Liechtenstein Alle 2A-1, a prestigious location opposite the Spanish embassy.[13] The Free India Centre soon attracted a number of Indian activists such as Abid Hasan, N.G. Swami and A.C.N. Nambiar. It was also at the centre that the Azad Hind Radio was established to transmit in short wave. A powerful transmitter in Holland beamed it to India, where these broadcasts were clandestinely heard by thousands. So, when a rumour spread in March 1942 that Subhas had been killed in an air crash in east Asia, Subhas

[12] Sitanshu Das, *Subhas: A Political Biography*, Rupa Publications India, 2001.
[13] John Jacob and Harindra Srivastava, *Netaji Subhas: The Tallest of Titans (But Betrayed and Belittled)*, Ess Ess Publications, 2000.

himself came on the radio and thundered, 'This is Subhas Chandra Bose, who is still alive, speaking to you over Azad Hind Radio ...'[14]

An effort was also made to recruit Indian soldiers held as prisoners of war into an 'Indian Legion'. This proceeded slowly, as most of the prisoners of war from north Africa were held in Italy and many of them feared the consequences for their families back in British India. Only about 4,000 signed up. The legion wore a German-style uniform with a tricolour emblem and a springing royal Bengal tiger stitched to the left sleeve.

Although the legion and the Free India Centre would have little impact on the course of the war, they had a lasting impact on Independent India. It was here that Subhas decided on Tagore's *Jana Gana Mana* as the national anthem. It was also here that the common Indian greeting 'Jai Hind!' was coined, and where Subhas came to be known as 'Netaji'.

Subhas was already thinking about how he could make his way to Japanese-held Asia when he finally got to meet Hitler on 24 May 1942. The meeting did not go well. Hitler lectured the Indian leader on the global war situation but did not commit to a declaration about Indian Independence. Bose then asked Hitler to withdraw racist references to Indians in *Mein Kampf*.[15] He most likely would not have known about Nazi death camps, but Bose was under no illusion that Hitler was anything but an unpredictable dictator. Therefore, this was a brave thing to bring up, even if it was hardly likely that the Führer was going to relent. The meeting came to an end after this.

Back in Asia, as Rashbehari's health deteriorated, he pressed for Subhas to take over the IIL. The Japanese began to

[14] *Ibid.*
[15] *Ibid.*

negotiate with the Germans on how to safely get him to east Asia. They initially debated flying him non-stop from Italy to Singapore, but decided it was too dangerous. Eventually it was decided that he would make his way to the Indian Ocean by submarine. The departure date was set for 8 February 1943. He decided to take along a young engineering student, Abid Hasan, as his personal secretary. All the arrangements were kept secret and even Hasan did not know where they were headed.

At dawn on the designated date, Commander Werner Musenberg received them at Kiel harbour on the Baltic and led them to the submarine U-180. The underwater craft made its way through the enemy-controlled waters of the North Atlantic and then around the southern tip of Africa. Meanwhile, the Japanese submarine I-29 surreptitiously made its way out of Penang harbour and headed for Madagascar. The two submarines made their rendezvous 400 nautical miles south-west of Madagascar on 26 April.

The problem was that the sea was too rough for the transfer. Things had still not improved by the next afternoon. Two audacious Germans now swam across to the Japanese submarine and rowed back with a lifeboat tied to a strong rope. The next morning, with the sea still rough, Subhas and his young assistant climbed into the boat and the Japanese reeled them in with the rope. Drenched, the two climbed into the Japanese vessel. The Indians were dropped off at Sabang, Sumatra, on 6 May. Yet again, Subhas Bose had pulled off an amazing getaway. A few days later, he was on a Japanese military aircraft bound for Tokyo.

Many of Subhas Bose's critics question his willingness to ally with the Axis powers. Indeed, he would go out of his way to address this in his radio broadcasts, where he explicitly stated that his mission to free India required difficult choices:

> 'In this fateful hour in Indian history, it would be a grievous mistake to be carried away by ideological considerations alone. The internal politics of Germany or Italy or Japan do not concern us—they are the concern of the people of those countries.' [16]

After arriving in Tokyo, Subhas spent several weeks getting to know key individuals in the Japanese political and military establishment. He then had multiple meetings with the Japanese premier Tojo. Unlike Hitler, Tojo was willing to publicly commit support for Indian Independence.

Subhas left for Singapore, along with Rashbehari, at the end of June. They received a rapturous welcome at Singapore's Kallang airport when they landed on 2 July. The INA presented a guard of honour while Indian civilians cheered loudly.

Two days later, members of the IIL assembled at the Cathay Theatre for a solemn ceremony, where Rashbehari Bose formally handed over the leadership to Subhas. It was a very emotional moment for everyone present. Rashbehari was not merely handing over the leadership of the IIL and the INA, but the baton of the cumulative efforts of the revolutionary movement over half a century.

The next morning, Subhas inspected the INA troops on the Padang field in the middle of Singapore. Dressed in military uniform, he took the salute from the steps of the Town Hall, as 12,000 INA soldiers marched past. In his address, he gave them their battle cry 'Dilli Chalo (Onward to Delhi)', evoking a vision of a victory parade at the Red Fort. A day later, Tojo also reviewed the Indian troops at the same location.

[16] As quoted in Sugata Bose, *His Majesty's Opponent*, Penguin India, 2013.

Subhas now embarked on a whirlwind of activity—making arrangements for the INA, meeting delegations of various civilian groups, negotiating with the Japanese and so on.

The Bengal Famine

As discussed previously, the British responded to the Quit India Movement and the feared Japanese invasion by unleashing an unprecedented regime of repression in India. After a series of particularly horrific incidents of police brutality in Bengal's Midnapur, Dr Syamaprasad Mookerjee, who had resigned from the Cabinet as the finance minister, wrote to Chief Minister Huq, who promised a senior-level inquiry. Governor Herbert was furious when he heard that an inquiry would be instituted, and vetoed it.

As if things were not bad enough, Bengal was hit by a cyclone on 16 October 1942. The storm and the accompanying tidal wave and floods devastated the fields, killed livestock, destroyed homes, washed away fish ponds and damaged food stock in southern Bengal, including in Midnapur. The district administration deliberately denied flood relief in those areas that were deemed 'disloyal'.

It was against this backdrop that the British decided to implement a 'Denial Policy'—a scorched-earth strategy aimed at denying food and other supplies to the advancing Japanese. Rice stocks in south and east Bengal were removed at a time when normal imports from Burma had been disrupted. Some of this was diverted towards feeding the amassing troops. However, the authorities simply destroyed tonnes of rice that could not be removed. At three river ports in east Bengal, large quantities of rice were just thrown into the water.

The policy was not restricted to foodgrains. Anything that could be useful to the Japanese was just commandeered or destroyed—boats, automobiles, cycles, radio sets and so on. Of the 66,700 boats in coastal Bengal, two-thirds were rendered inoperable or taken away. The remaining operable vessels were pressed into government service for transporting supplies needed for the war effort. Thus, as the famine took root, the poor peasants were not even able to catch fish, a very important part of the local diet. Combined with the rice-denial policy and the cyclone, the conditions were ripe for a catastrophe.

By the end of 1942, Calcutta and other urban centres witnessed a sharp increase in famished peasants wandering around begging for food. Across Bengal, people were starting to die of starvation. Concerns were raised by Nalinaksha Sanyal, now the official chief whip of the INC in the Bengal provincial assembly, but were dismissed. In a caustic speech, Dr Sanyal pointed out that even when government rules required food stocks to be released, the bureaucrats made sure that there were no bullock carts and workers to help move them.[17] This is why it is more than fair to state that the Bengal Famine of 1943 was deliberate and man-made.

By April 1943, the news of a famine in Bengal had reached both Delhi and London. Civil Supplies Minister Suhrawardy continued to claim that there was no major shortage of foodgrains in Bengal and that it was a minor localized problem caused by 'hoarding' by traders. As a telling reflection of racial bias, the Indians were accused of hoarding, while European-owned establishments were officially told to 'stockpile' food.

Even when it was obvious by mid-1943 that millions of people were starving, colonial authorities continued to minimize the issue and blame the people. Prime Minister Churchill was direct about what he thought of Indians in general and Hindus in particular: *'I hate Indians. They are a beastly people with a beastly religion.'*[18]

Despite wartime censorship, Subhas Bose learnt of the famine raging in his home province in mid-1943. He immediately conferred with Japanese officials and Burmese leaders, and offered to send a large shipment of rice from Burma. The British rejected the offer, possibly because it would have further increased Subhas' popularity. The War Cabinet even turned down offers of help from Australia on grounds that it would divert critical shipping.

The food-supply situation began to improve by November 1943, as the new harvest came and the government machinery finally started mobilizing some relief supplies. By then, it is estimated that three million people had died in the famine.

[17] Bikramjit De, 'Imperial Governance and the Challenges of War: Management of Food Supplies in Bengal, 1943-44', Studies in History, Sage Publications, 2006.
[18] Madhusree Mukerjee, *Churchill's Secret War: The British Empire and the Ravaging of India during World War II*, Penguin India, 2010.

The Flag in Moirang

By the time Subhas Bose landed in Singapore, the tide of the war had already turned. The Germans had been pushed back from Stalingrad and the Japanese navy had been decimated at Midway. Even as he inspected the INA troops, therefore, he would have known that the chances of an outright military victory were eroding. However, the old revolutionary objective of triggering a full-fledged revolt in the Indian armed forces was still very much possible. The idea was to create an unstoppable vortex that would trigger a revolution in the British Indian Army as well as the general population.

In mid-October 1943, Subhas threw himself into writing a 'Proclamation of Independence'. He was working non-stop at this time to build up the INA and create the architecture of a provisional government. S.A. Ayer would later recall that when Bose had finished writing the draft proclamation, he turned to his aides and asked them if they knew what had happened to the signatories of the Irish proclamation of independence—they had all been shot dead. With a laugh, he added that the same may happen to the signatories of this one.[19]

On 21 October 1943, a large IIL meeting was called at the Cathay Theatre, where Subhas Bose announced the formation of the Provisional Government of Free India *(Arzi Hukumat-e-Azad Hind)*. Subhas Bose was sworn in as the head of state and premier; Rashbehari was given the title of supreme adviser. None of the witnesses would have been in any doubt that this was a historic moment. Within days, the provisional government was recognized by Japan, Germany, Italy, Croatia,

---

[19] Sugata Bose, *His Majesty's Opponent*, Penguin India, 2013.

Thailand, Burma, the Philippines and Manchukuo. President Eamon de Valera of the Irish Free State also sent a personal note of congratulations to Subhas. Before the end of the month, the Japanese government had handed over the Andaman and Nicobar Islands to the provisional government. Given that the Andamans were where generations of revolutionaries had been imprisoned and tortured, this was emotionally charged symbolism. Thus, the Provisional Government of Free India now had international recognition, an army and de jure control over territory. It would later issue its own currency.

Subhas was keen that the INA be deployed soon in Burma as part of an invasion of the Indian mainland. The Japanese, however, dithered as they were distracted by developments in the Pacific. Moreover, they were unsure of the fighting preparedness of the INA, including that of a newly recruited women's unit called the Rani of Jhansi regiment. Even as he waited for the Japanese to make a decision, Subhas visited the Cellular Jail in Port Blair in December. At a press conference, he explained the significance of his visit: *'Like the Bastille in Paris, which was liberated first during the French Revolution, setting free political prisoners, the Andamans, where our patriots suffered much, is the first to be liberated in India's fight for Independence.'*[20]

In anticipation of the main thrust into India's North-East, a small covert operations group was sent by submarine to the Kathiawar coast. They were equipped with sophisticated wireless sets to communicate with the INA. Their mission was to connect with the remaining revolutionary groups and instigate them to carry out guerrilla attacks across British India. The group was successful in connecting with several people, including members of the Bose family, but they seem

[20] John Jacob and Harindra Srivastava, *Netaji Subhas: The Tallest of Titans (But Betrayed and Belittled)*, Ess Ess Publications, 2000.

to have been too trusting of contacts with communist links. Bhagat Ram Talwar, for instance, passed on all information to his party leadership, who, in turn, gave it to British intelligence. As a result, the members of the covert operations were arrested over the course of 1944.

In January 1944, the INA moved north to Burma and established a new headquarters in Rangoon (now Yangon). When the Japanese Imperial Army commenced their offensive against Imphal and Kohima in the second week of March, the INA regiments were deployed along with them. Around 84,000 Japanese troops, plus 12,000 INA soldiers faced 155,000 British, British Indian, West African and American troops.[21]

The Japanese–INA forces entered Manipur on 18 March 1944 and initially made rapid progress. They were travelling light as their tactics depended on speed and hoped to capture enough supplies from the Allies to sustain their momentum. They were accompanied by a group of nationalist Meitei Manipuris led by L. Guno Singh, who had joined the INA in Rangoon. This group quickly established contact with local organizations such as the Nikhil Manipuri Mahasabha and Praja Sammelani. Similarly, contact was established with Kuki tribal chiefs to elicit their support.

A few days later, the Praja Sammelani smuggled handbills into Imphal, appealing to the Manipuris to rise up against the British. Many young Meitis, including P. Tomal Singh, L. Irabot Singh, O. Keinya Devi and M. Randhoni Devi responded to the appeal. They quietly sneaked out of Imphal and headed towards the small town of Moirang, which lay in the path of the approaching Indo-Japanese forces.

The Allies, meanwhile, were forced to retreat. As part of the scorched-earth 'Denial Policy', they burnt down food

---

[21] Sugata Bose, *His Majesty's Opponent*, Penguin India, 2013.

stocks and even houses along the path of retreat. On the morning of 14 April, when Manipuris were celebrating their New Year festival, the activists in Moirang heard that Indo-Japanese troops had reached a village just 5 kilometres away. They immediately went there to welcome them. At 5 p.m. that evening, an INA column led by Colonel Shaukat Ali Malik and Japanese troops led by Captain Ito entered Moirang. They were welcomed by M. Koireng Singh.

They next proceeded to Moirang Kangla, a sacred citadel where local kings were traditionally crowned. It was here that Malik raised the INA flag—a tricolour with a springing tiger. This was the first time that the Provisional Government of Free India had taken control of territory on the Indian mainland. He then gave a rousing speech (translated into Manipuri by Koireng Singh):

> 'Our commitment is to march to Delhi and unfurl the tricolor flag at Red Fort. Many have died on the way to reach here, and many will die on our way to Delhi.'[22]

[22] *Ibid.*

During their retreat, the British commanders had burnt down many of the houses in Moirang. Two of the surviving houses were converted into field hospitals. A house belonging to Hemam Nilamani Singh was converted into the local INA headquarters. The activists then organized food supplies for the Indo-Japanese forces. This was not easy, as the Allies had destroyed whatever they could find, but surrounding villages generously sent in enough provisions for some 10,000 troops for three months. The British were aware that the locals were helping the Indo-Japanese forces. Moirang was declared an 'enemy zone' and 'shoot at sight' orders were issued against known activists.

Through April and May, battles raged in many places in Manipur. In a major battle at Lokpaching (Red Hill) during 25–30 May, both sides suffered heavy casualties in fierce hand-to-hand combat. The British, nonetheless, were able to stall the advance towards Imphal.

The advance towards Kohima was similarly quick in the initial phase. Subhas Bose would even stay for a few days at Ruzazho village (in Phek district, Nagaland) while visiting the front. He must have made quite an impression on the local tribes as they sing folk songs in his honour to this day.

Unfortunately, here, too, the momentum stalled, with heavy casualties to both sides. The Allied garrison in Kohima had received advance warning and hastily dug into defensive positions along a mile-long ridge. The assistant district commissioner's bungalow fell along the ridge and the attached garden and tennis court exchanged hands several times in the course of an eyeball-to-eyeball confrontation. Known as the Battle of the Tennis Court, it marks the turning point in the campaign. The Japanese lost the tennis court and were then forced back from Kohima by mid-May. The Allies were exhausted but had held on to Kohima and Imphal.

The Indo-Japanese forces had lost their momentum. They were still a potent force, but the monsoon arrived early that year. India's North-East is among the wettest places on Earth and the Indo-Japanese strategy of travelling light backfired. The supply routes through the jungles of Burma quickly became mired in impassable mud. Short on food, medicine and ammunition, both the INA and the Japanese soldiers were trapped in their waterlogged trenches. Disease took a heavy toll on the exhausted troops. In the middle of the deteriorating situation, a senior commander, Major B.J.S. Garewal, defected to the British and took crucial details of INA positions with him.[23]

Even before Subhas Bose met his commanders in Mandalay in September, he would have realized that the situation was difficult. It was made worse by the fact that the Japanese were waging a desperate defence in the Pacific and were in no position to spare their military aircraft. This left the skies open to the Allies for strafing and bombing Indo-Japanese positions with impunity. The tin roof of the INA headquarters in Moirang still has the bullet holes from aerial strafing. Hundreds of Manipuri civilians were also killed from Allied bombing in Moirang and surrounding villages. Many of the Manipuri activists joined the INA as it retreated into Burma.

Bose had hoped to be able to hold a line along the Irrawaddy river. By February 1945, however, the INA soldiers were fighting a war that they knew could not be won. The Axis powers were now being defeated everywhere across the world, supplies were running short and the Allies were on the

[23] Sugata Bose, *His Majesty's Opponent,* Penguin India, 2013.

offensive. And yet, despite occasional desertions, the INA held together as a fighting unit. The Indians fought courageously at Mount Popa in early April against overwhelming odds before being forced to abandon the position. By mid-May, however, the Allies had captured three key field commanders—Prem Kumar Sehgal, Shah Nawaz Khan and Gurbaksh Singh Dhillon.

Meanwhile, Rashbehari Bose passed away from cerebral haemorrhage in Tokyo on 21 January 1945. He was fifty-eight and died before seeing his beloved motherland liberated. His son Masahide was with him in his last moments, but returned to the front shortly afterwards. He was killed in Okinawa on 15 June.

Atom bombs were dropped on Hiroshima and Nagasaki on 6 and 9 August 1945. The Japanese surrendered on 15 August. Subhas Bose was in Singapore at that time. His chief concern was to make sure that the INA soldiers were paid and that the 500 women of the Rani of Jhansi regiment were sent back to their families.

Subhas now had rapidly diminishing options, and he discussed them with his Cabinet. It was almost certain that the British would arrest him and treat him as a war criminal. Leaving behind Major General M.Z. Kiani in charge of the remnants of the INA, he flew to Bangkok, and then to Saigon (now Ho Chi Minh City) and Da Nang before landing in Taipei on 18 August.

What happened next is a matter of controversy. The official narrative is that his plane crashed while taking off for Tokyo and that Subhas died of severe burns. Right from the beginning this was disputed by those who believed (or hoped) that he had staged yet another escape. In any case, he was not seen in public after 18 August 1945, although his long shadow would fall on subsequent events.

The INA Trials

With the Japanese defeated and their leader missing, the remaining INA units were forced to surrender. The British decided to make an example of the 'traitors' through a series of high-profile trials at the Red Fort in Delhi, followed by exemplary punishments. The thinking was presumably driven by the idea that the Indian population could yet again be frightened into submission, as had happened after the Revolt of 1857–58 and again after the First World War. This time, however, they miscalculated. Due to wartime censorship, the general public had only dimly known of the INA and had not been aware of the scale of its operations, the bold adventures of its leader and the fact that an army of liberation had actually managed to enter India. By making these facts known widely through the trials, the British inadvertently stirred up passions across the country.

The INA veterans were accused of 'waging war against the King-Emperor', which was punishable by death or transportation for life, and a hefty fine (usually confiscation of all property). The first three officers chosen to be tried in November 1945 were Shah Nawaz Khan, Prem Kumar Sehgal and Gurbaksh Singh Dhillon. The Congress organized a strong defence team led by the renowned lawyers Tej Bahadur Sapru and Bhulabhai Desai. Interestingly, Nehru donned his barrister's gown after thirty years to join the team, although he did not play an active role in the proceedings.

The line of defence was an interesting one. Against the accusations of disloyalty and treachery, the defence argued that the Provisional Government of Free India was a recognized and legitimate government and that the INA was its regular army. The Allies had themselves recognized several governments in exile, such as that of Poland and France. Therefore, the INA veterans should be treated as prisoners of war and could not be considered traitors.

Many of the undertrials were housed in Salimgarh Fort, a smaller military fort adjoining the Red Fort. This fort was long used by the Mughals as a high-security prison for royals and high nobility. Following the Revolt of 1857, several high-profile prisoners, including Bahadur Shah Zafar, had been held here. The use of this fort as a prison for the INA veterans was filled with symbolism for both sides. The trio of Khan, Dhillon and Sehgal, however, were kept separately in a room built into a medieval *baoli* (stepwell) within the Red Fort.

The Red Fort trials were followed in minute detail in the press and the first three accused officers became instant heroes. There were demonstrations held across the country in solidarity with their cause. The mood did not merely impact the civilian population but also those serving in the British Indian armed forces—the same men who had fought against the INA just months earlier!

It should be remembered that the British Indian Army held large swathes of Asia in late 1945, including Burma, Indonesia, Malaya, Singapore and even southern Vietnam. Indian troops were also stationed in the Middle East. They soon realized that they were being used to control the locals in each country until their respective European colonizers could come back from the war. For instance, British Indian troops were used to fight Indonesian freedom fighters in pitched battles in Surabaya in November 1945, even as the Dutch prepared to reoccupy the islands. Thousands of Indonesians were killed, but a couple of hundred British

Indian troops were also killed. Resentment was so high that the British commanders feared that some of the Indian units would switch sides. Thus, the change in mood in the British Indian armed forces was no small matter on the international stage. By the end of 1945, the senior echelons of the British establishment were becoming aware of the precarious position. It is not surprising, therefore, that when Sehgal, Dhillon and Khan were given life sentences, Commander-in-Chief Claude Auchinleck was forced to commute the sentences and release them.

The Naval Mutiny [24]

The Royal Indian Navy had its origins in the Bombay Marine, which was set up as a local auxiliary to support the Royal Navy against the Maratha navy in the eighteenth century. It was formalized into the Royal Indian Marine in 1892 and participated in the First World War, mostly for the transportation of Indian troops to the Middle East and for coastal patrols. In 1934, it was upgraded to the Royal Indian Navy (RIN), but remained a modest force until the eve of the Second World War in 1939, with two sloops, one survey ship, four escort patrol vessels and thirty-three auxiliary boats. By the end of the Second World War, however, it had dramatically expanded to 132 ships, including gunboats and frigates.

The staff strength of the navy similarly expanded. In 1939, the RIN had merely 212 officers—and most of them were British. By 1945, the number had gone up to 2,852 and included 949 Indians. Similarly, the number of ratings (sailors) jumped from 1,475 to around 28,000 during this period.

[24] This section has relied on a number of sources, including Lt Cdr G.D. Sharma, *Untold Story: 1946 Naval Mutiny: Last War of Independence*, Vij Books, 2015; Pramod Kapoor, *1946: Last War of Independence*, Roli Books, 2022; and contemporary news reports.

In late 1945, a large number of these sailors were being demobilized and were sent to camps in Bombay for the process. However, with the war over, the British authorities had lost interest in them, and the camps were severely overcrowded. There were inadequate arrangements for food and housing. Two-thirds of the ratings did not even have cots to sleep on and were forced to sleep cheek-by-jowl on the floor. What made it worse was the attitude of the British officers, who met all complaints by hurling racist slurs at them.

Huddled in these crowded camps, the RIN sailors followed the INA trials with a growing sense of disillusionment. A small group of relatively educated ratings, including Madan Singh, Mohammad Shuaib Khan, Rishi Dev Puri and Balai Chandra Dutt, began to meet regularly to discuss the situation. They called themselves the 'Azad Hindi', a direct reference to the INA and Subhas Bose's provisional government. They decided to carry out an act of revolt during the Navy Day celebrations on 1 December 1945. In addition to senior military and government officials, several prominent citizens had been invited. The event was to be held at *HMIS Talwar*, a shore establishment in Bombay's Colaba area, which was used by the navy's signals corps for training and operations.

The midnight-to-4 a.m. slot for sentry duty was not popular, so the Azad Hindis easily managed to get one of their own on duty. A small group led by Dutt and Puri gained entry into *Talwar*. As a senior telegraphist in the RIN, Dutt was already familiar with the facility. The buildings had been spruced up for the Navy Day event, but by 4 a.m., the group had prominently painted the walls with slogans such as 'Quit India', 'Revolt Now', 'Down with the Imperialists' and 'Kill the British'. When these were discovered the next day, the RIN became the laughing stock of the city.[25]

[25] Pramod Kapoor, *1946: Last War of Independence*, Roli Books, 2022.

The British were unable to identify the culprits, so they responded by putting Commander Arthur Frederick King, a racist with a reputation for toughness, in charge of *Talwar*. They also dismissed and sent away Puri, whom they suspected despite lack of any direct evidence.

The commander-in-chief of British forces in India, Field Marshal Claude Auchinleck, was expected to visit Bombay in early February 1946. King managed to convince the higher authorities that holding an event in *Talwar* would be a good way to showcase the re-imposition of order. Thus, it was decided that Auchinleck would deliver a speech at the facility on 2 February. A stage was erected and the buildings repainted.

Not surprisingly, security was very tight this time. However, Dutt had a legitimate reason to be there, as he was from the signals unit. He stayed back overnight and painted 'JAI HIND' on the stage built for the commander-in-chief. He also pasted a large number of revolutionary posters all over the yard. As can be imagined, there was pandemonium when these were discovered at first light, just hours before the speech.

Dutt may have escaped a second time for lack of evidence, but he had been seen taking a bottle of gum from the wireless room. His locker was checked, and it yielded copies of a revolutionary pamphlet and several books. He was immediately thrown into solitary confinement.

When the bugles were sounded for assembly at 8.45 a.m. on 18 February 1946, none of the ratings at *Talwar* showed up. They had earlier refused to eat breakfast as they deemed the food unfit for consumption. When King arrived at the facility, nationalist slogans were raised. Moreover, since these were signals men, they telegraphed their strike to the ships and other shore establishments. By evening, a mutiny was rapidly spreading across the RIN.

Next morning, the British realized that they had a full-fledged revolt on their hands. Ten thousand naval ratings left their barracks and demobilization camps and marched to the harbour. This was an organized group that had fought together. Within hours they had taken over two more shore establishments, Castle Barracks and Fort Barracks. Next, they took over, one by one, the RIN ships in the harbour: *Berar, Moti, Neelum, Jumna* and others. Officers, both Indian and British, were confined to their cabins even as the sailors took control. They pulled down the Union Jack and unfurled the Congress and Muslim League flags. The CPI flag was added shortly thereafter. The ratings did not want to be seen as politically aligned to any specific party.

A large group of ratings gathered at the *Talwar* by noon. A central strike committee was formed with leading signalman M.S. Khan as president and telegraphist Madan Singh as vice president. They also renamed RIN as the Indian National Navy—again, an obvious reference to the INA. All of these developments were quickly transmitted to the ships and shore establishments controlled by the ratings. The committee also presented its demands, which included an immediate release of all political prisoners and INA veterans, independent inquiry into the large number of deaths from police/military firing in the previous few years and an immediate withdrawal of Indian troops from Southeast Asia and the Middle East.

With the situation spiralling out of control, Rear Admiral Rattray called for army troops to re-establish control. Troops from the Mahratta regiment were sent to Castle Barracks. Known today as *INS Angre*, it is a fortified complex built originally by the Portuguese in the sixteenth century and then further enhanced by the East India Company in the subsequent centuries. The Mahrattas took up positions and set up machine-gun posts outside Castle Barracks by mid-afternoon. The ratings responded by arming themselves from the naval armoury and setting up defences. They also started to prime the big guns on the ships.

By the morning of 21 February, the mutiny included 20,000 ratings, 78 ships and 21 shore establishments. Moreover, the revolt had spread beyond Bombay. In Karachi, for instance, the sailors took over two ships, *HMIS Hindustan* and *Travancore,* and the shore establishment *HMIS Himalaya.* Calcutta also witnessed a strike.

Back at Castle Barracks in Bombay, the Mahratta brigade was ordered to open fire. The sailors retaliated. An officer who had climbed on top of the Reserve Bank of India building was shot down. This led to an exchange of fire until the British commanders realized that the Mahrattas were deliberately making sure that they were not hitting targets. Indian troops were quickly replaced by those of the Leicestershire Regiment.

The British next ordered the Royal Indian Air Force (RIAF) to get ready to bomb the ships. The airmen flatly refused and themselves went on strike. A RIAF squadron told to proceed immediately to Bombay was grounded in Jodhpur when all the planes mysteriously developed engine problems.

With European troops now surrounding the naval establishments, the attack began in earnest, with armoured vehicles and machine guns. A squadron of Royal Air Force Mosquitoes flew over the harbour to intimidate the rebels. The sailors fought back. *HMIS Punjab* fired 120 rounds from its twelve-pounder at government forces on the shore, followed by firing from its anti-aircraft guns.

Karachi also witnessed similar developments when the Gurkha and Baloch soldiers refused to fire on the sailors and had to be replaced by European troops. As their authority over the Indian armed forces crumbled, it was obvious to the British authorities that they were no longer in a position to sustain their colonial occupation of the country. Thus, even as battles raged on the streets of Bombay, British Prime Minister Clement Attlee announced the visit of a three-member Cabinet Mission to start the process for an 'early realization of full self-government in India'.[26] The moment had finally arrived!

By the time news of Attlee's announcement arrived, the whole city of Bombay was in full revolt. A large number of students, factory workers and other common citizens had gathered in support of the RIN ratings. They quickly established a system of supplying food to the sailors holed up in different parts of the city. The British responded by ordering the troops to fire on the protesters. Between 400 and 700 were killed, and 1,500 wounded. The crackdown did not deter large gatherings of protesters in Madras,

[26] *Ibid.*

Visakhapatnam, Calcutta, Ahmedabad, Karachi and other cities across the subcontinent.

The Naval Revolt had triggered what seemed like an unstoppable wave, but the RIN ratings knew that they could not sustain this for too long. Not only were they surrounded, they were also not in a position to use their big guns on the city without risking large-scale civilian casualties. A political solution was needed. Eventually, it became clear that the bulk of the political establishment was not going to support the revolt. The rebels were disappointed when they realized they were being advised to surrender unconditionally. Some such as Madan Singh were in favour of fighting to the bitter end, but the ratings eventually surrendered on 24 February. Despite the assurances of the Congress leaders that the ratings would not be victimized if they laid down arms, hundreds were arrested and imprisoned.

Just like the Revolt of 1857, this one, too, had been crushed, but it was obvious that the game had changed. The INA and the Naval Revolt had irrevocably broken the Indian soldier's loyalty to the British crown. This had major consequences for the empire. A glance at the newspapers from that time show that British troops were fighting independence movements across the world.

The chain of events triggered by Attlee's announcement of a Cabinet Mission led India to become independent on 15 August 1947, just eighteen months after the Naval Mutiny.

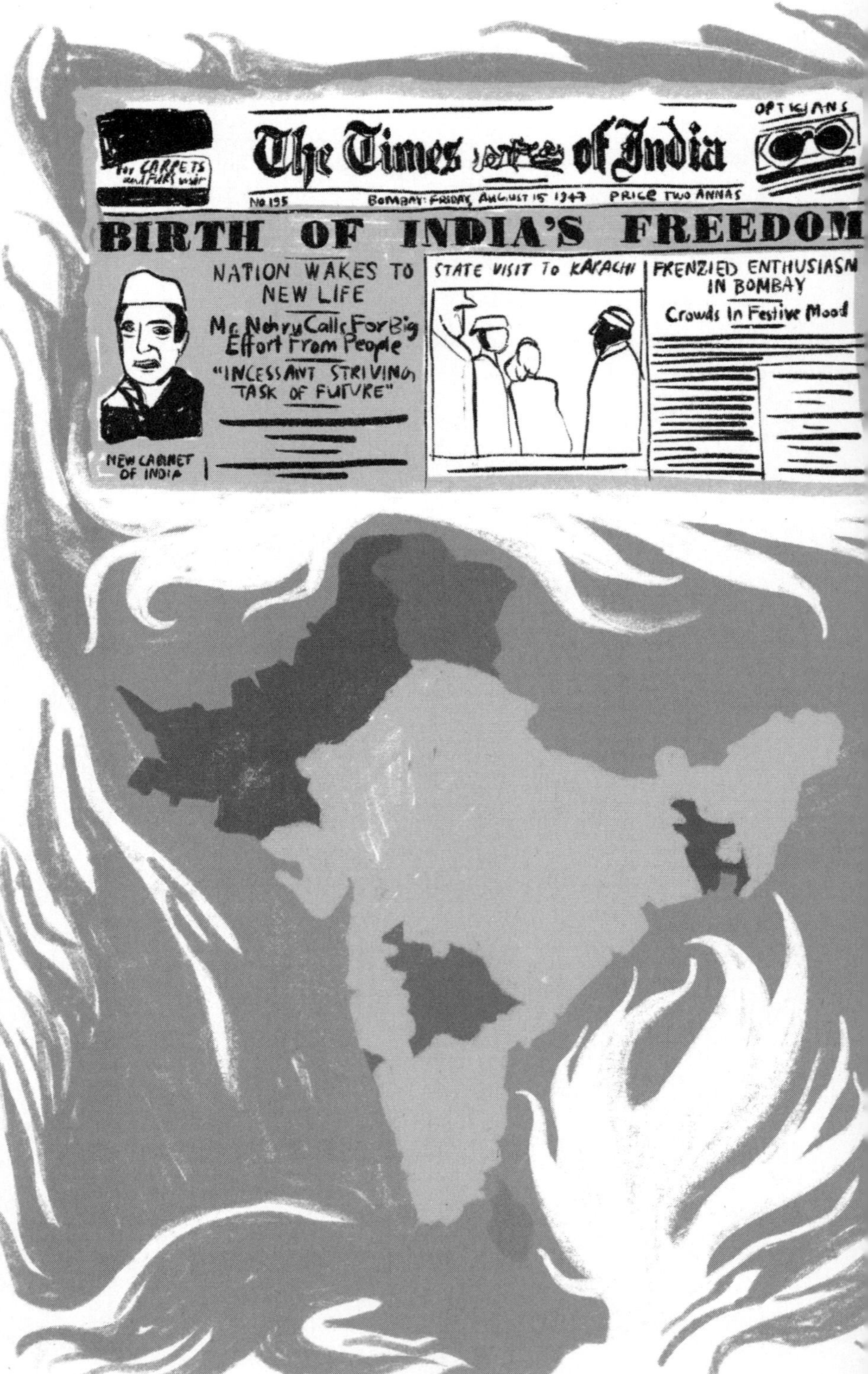

for CARPETS
OPTICIANS
The Times of India
No 195
BOMBAY: FRIDAY, AUGUST 15 1947
PRICE TWO ANNAS
BIRTH OF INDIA'S FREEDOM
NATION WAKES TO NEW LIFE
Mr Nehru Calls For Big Effort From People
"INCESSANT STRIVING TASK OF FUTURE"
NEW CABINET OF INDIA
STATE VISIT TO KARACHI
FRENZIED ENTHUSIASM IN BOMBAY
Crowds In Festive Mood

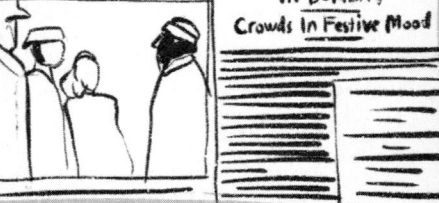

Epilogue

After centuries of foreign occupation, India finally became free on 15 August 1947. This should have been a moment of unalloyed joy for the revolutionaries and their families, who had sacrificed so much for this moment. But this was not to be. Independence also meant the Partition of India, specifically that of Punjab and Bengal. Places such as Lahore and Dhaka, which had been important hubs of India's freedom struggle, were no longer be part of the country. In one stroke, millions of Indians became foreigners in their own land. Hundreds of thousands faced loss of life and property. The revolutionaries had repeatedly felt let down by the political leadership, but this was arguably the greatest betrayal of all.

While the revolutionaries were left with no option but to support the Partition, a few individuals worked desperately to prevent the situation from worsening further. Dr Syamaprasad Mookerjee, together with Nalinaksha Sanyal, convinced enough Congress legislators to vote for the partition of Bengal to prevent Bengal from becoming an independent state with a Bengali Hindu minority or ending up with Pakistan. As the country's leading transportation economist at that time, Nalinaksha made the case that the main railway lines and the river system feeding Calcutta port had to be retained in India for economic viability. The Radcliffe Commission accepted the arguments. This is why Murshidabad, Maldah and most of Nadia district stayed with India. This is how the new state of West Bengal was born.

Independence did not prove to be kind to the other community that had provided so many revolutionaries—the Maharashtrian Brahmins. A member of the community, Nathuram Godse, assassinated Gandhi in Delhi on 30 January 1948.

This unleashed a wave of mob violence against the Brahmin community across Maharashtra. Estimates vary, but thousands of homes and businesses were burnt down and hundreds were killed. What made it worse was that the government of Independent India deliberately suppressed information about the 1948 pogrom—it is spoken in whispers to this day. This was unfortunate, as no lessons were learnt, and the sequence of events was repeated during the anti-Sikh riots that followed the assassination of Indira Gandhi in 1984. The assassination of both the Gandhis was wrong, but so was the mob violence against whole communities that followed.

The mobs particularly targeted the Savarkar brothers, as they were suspected of being directly involved in the assassination plot. A large mob of Congress party workers turned up at the home of Narayanrao Savarkar and beat him mercilessly. Narayan suffered severe head injuries from which he never recovered and, after more than a year in hospital, died from brain haemorrhage.

The mob then went to look for Vinayak Savarkar at his house in Dadar. They were delayed long enough by a couple of supporters to allow the police to arrive. This likely saved the family from meeting the same fate as Narayanrao. Vinayak Savarkar was arrested on suspicion of being part of the Gandhi-assassination plot. This led to yet another historic trial at Red Fort in 1948, where he was tried along with Nathuram Godse and several others. Godse had always admitted to killing Gandhi and was hanged in November 1949. The case against Savarkar was weak, and he was acquitted.

Ullaskar Dutt had been a key member of Barin Ghosh's original Anushilan Samiti. Before he was arrested in 1908, Ullaskar was engaged to be married to his college sweetheart Lila. Readers will recall that he was so severely tortured in the

Cellular Jail that he almost lost his mind. He was subsequently sent to a mental asylum in Madras for a long and painful recovery. It is said that through it all, it was the thought of Lila that kept him going. When Ullaskar finally went looking for Lila, he discovered that she, unaware of what had happened to him, had married someone else. Ullaskar returned to the revolutionary life and was jailed again in the early 1930s. By the time India gained Independence, he is said to have become a recluse in a village in East Bengal. However, when he heard that Lila was a widow and paralyzed from the waist down, he located and finally married her and looked after her in her last years.

Bina Das had been sentenced to nine years in prison for shooting at Bengal Governor Stanley Jackson in 1932. After her early release in 1939, she continued to participate in the freedom movement. She became a teacher and married a fellow revolutionary. After independence, she served for a term in the West Bengal legislative assembly. However, after the death of her husband in the mid-1980s, she became a recluse and shifted to Varanasi to engage in spiritual pursuits. She later moved to Rishikesh and died there.

After participating in Ghadarite activities in Japan and North America, and then fighting the British in Persia during the First World War, Pandurang Khankhoje knew he could not return to India. He headed to Mexico, where he became a famous agricultural expert. Indeed, his innovations in farm technology, initially in wheat and maize, transformed the sector worldwide. He developed rust-resistant, frost-resistant and drought-resistant varieties of wheat that greatly benefited global food production. These innovations eventually found their way to India in the form of the Green Revolution in the late 1960s and 1970s. Khankhoje next studied the indigenous plants of Central America. This led to the discovery of plant-derived steroids and hormones. His collaboration with Vicks Chemical Company led to innovations in mint-oil extraction that are still used. Khankhoje moved to Nagpur with his family in 1955 and spent the rest of his life in India. He passed away in January 1987.

One of the ironies of history is that Independent India refused to rehabilitate the INA veterans and RIN rebels. Not only were they not taken back into the armed forces, they were not even given recognition as freedom fighters until the 1970s. The justification given was that it would impact 'discipline' in the armed forces. The more likely reason is that many colonial-era officials, both British and Indian, continued to occupy positions of power in newly Independent India. Not surprisingly, they were not sympathetic to the revolutionaries in general and the INA/RIN veterans in particular. Many readers will be shocked to learn that the first four admirals to head the Indian Navy after 1947 were all British. It was only in 1958 that the first Indian, Admiral Ram Das Khatri, headed the Indian Navy. Even Commander Arthur King, whose racist behaviour had triggered the RIN revolt, was offered a senior role by the government of free India, although he preferred to return to the United Kingdom.

Although the government of Pakistan did not re-absorb the RIN rebels either, Jinnah enthusiastically welcomed Muslim INA veterans into the army. Some senior commanders of the INA, such as Mohammad Zaman Kiani and Habibur Rahman, fought for the Pakistani cause in the first Indo-Pak War of 1947–48 over Jammu and Kashmir. Thus, the irony is that the only veterans of Subhas Bose's INA to participate in war after independence ended up fighting against Azad Hind.

The better-educated RIN ratings managed to make a life for themselves after their dismissal. B.C. Dutt tried his hand at journalism at the Free Press Journal, where he shared a cabin with a young cartoonist named Balasaheb Thackeray. However, after three years, he switched to advertising and spent two decades at Lintas. M.S. Khan, who had served as the president of the RIN strike committee, is known to have gone to Gujranwala, now in Pakistan. However, nothing is known of what happened to him after Partition. His deputy Madan Singh helped Biju Patnaik, the famous Odiya politician-activist, set up Kalinga Airways in 1948. When the airline was nationalized in 1952 as part of Prime Minister Nehru's socialist policies, he ended up in London, working for British Overseas Airlines Corporation (now British Airways).

Since almost none of their top leaders survived till independence, the revolutionary movement did not hold together as a united force. Nonetheless, a few individuals did have successful political careers. The most successful survivor of the armed struggle was Shah Nawaz Khan, part of the trio from the INA trials. Although most of his family shifted to Pakistan, he stayed back in India and represented the Meerut constituency four times in the Lok Sabha as a member of the INC; he even became a minister. His best remembered contribution is serving as the chairman of a commission to investigate the disappearance of Subhas Bose. His findings are hotly debated to this day.

Mairembam Koireng Singh, who had welcomed the INA into Moirang, became the first chief minister of Manipur. Hemam Nilamani Singh, whose house was used by the INA as the Forward headquarters, became the deputy education minister of the state.

The RSS had been very active at the time of Partition and played an important role in providing support and rehabilitation for Hindu refugees pouring into the country from Pakistan. This allowed it to significantly expand its network. However, this growth was disrupted when it was briefly banned after Gandhi's assassination, and thousands of RSS members were jailed. After the ban was lifted, the RSS decided to help Syamaprasad Mookerjee, now a cabinet minister, set up a new party after he left the Hindu Mahasabha. A new party named Bharatiya Jana Sangh (BJS) was formed in 1951. The party did moderately well in the next few decades, but was never a threat to the hegemony of the Congress.

The RSS itself, meanwhile, turned its attention to the enclaves still controlled by the Portuguese on the west coast of India—Daman, Diu, Goa, Dadra and Nagar Haveli. In 1954, it formed an alliance with two parties operating in Portuguese India—the National Movement Liberation Organization and the Azad Gomantak Dal. On 2 August 1954, a small group of just a hundred volunteers stormed Dadra and Nagar Haveli and took over the enclaves. The Portuguese officials and the contingent of 175 soldiers were completely taken by surprise and they surrendered without a fight. For a short while, Dadra and Nagar Haveli were independent countries in the eyes of international law, until they were absorbed into the Republic of India.

The freedom movement in the remaining Portuguese-held enclaves was ramped up. The Portuguese responded by reinforcing their position. On 15 August 1955, large protests were organized by the alliance. The Portuguese police opened fire and killed thirty protesters (several from the RSS). Hundreds were arrested and put in prison. An armed resistance began to take shape. The escalating situation finally forced a reluctant

Nehru to order a military takeover of Goa, Daman and Diu in December 1961.

The RSS and BJS remained a significant presence in India's sociopolitical landscape in the 1960s and 1970s. When Prime Minister Indira Gandhi suspended democracy and declared the Emergency in 1975, tens of thousands of RSS volunteers and members of affiliated entities were thrown into jail. The organization's origins in the revolutionary movement, however, allowed it to continue functioning underground. The friendships built in jail and clandestine political activity welded together a network that would eventually flower in the 1990s. Narendra Modi and Arun Jaitley were products of this period. Inadvertently, Indira Gandhi had turned this offshoot of the revolutionary movement into a potent political force.

In 1977, the BJS merged into the Janata Party—a rainbow alliance that ousted Indira Gandhi. The new government did not last as it lacked a coherent ideology and leadership, and Indira Gandhi returned to power in 1980. With the Janata Party disintegrating, the remnants of the BJS were reconvened as the Bharatiya Janata Party (BJP). After a shaky start, the party gathered steam and anchored coalition governments under Prime Minister Atal Bihari Vajpayee between 1998 and 2004. It then returned in 2014 with a full majority under Prime Minister Narendra Modi, and then again in 2019. Thus, after many twists and turns, this particular derivative of the revolutionary movement became the dominant political force in India in the twenty-first century.

In December 1958, the surviving revolutionaries organized a large conference in Delhi under the chairmanship of Bhupendra Nath Dutta, the younger brother of Swami Vivekananda. Around 400 delegates attended the event and included representatives from every generation of the movement: Barin Ghosh, Sohan Singh Bhakna, Jogesh Chatterjee and others. Prime Minister Nehru even invited them for tea at his official residence.

The attendees recalled many of the great freedom fighters who had not survived; a special cheer went up for Rashbehari Bose, who had been involved for almost the entire duration of the movement. One of the topics that was discussed at the conference was the fact that, even by the 1950s, the official narrative about the freedom movement had systematically edited out the contributions of the armed resistance.

The revolutionaries were never fully forgotten by Indians despite official antipathy. The events were too recent and their activities still vividly remembered in collective memory. The memories of individual revolutionaries were kept alive by friends, family and their native towns/villages. However, they were systematically reduced to no more than a passing reference in school textbooks and national events. Thus, generations of Indians were sold a narrative that the contributions of the revolutionaries were no more than random acts without coherent objectives, and consequently as having no impact on the course of events. As we have seen, this is clearly not true. The story of the revolutionaries is essential to understanding the INC itself.

The good news is that in recent years, there has been renewed interest in the history of the armed resistance. Long-forgotten revolutionaries have started popping up in social media and popular culture. In 2019, four of the last remaining INA veterans were driven down Raj Path as part of the Republic Day Parade. The Indian Navy celebrated the RIN revolt as a float at the annual event in 2022. In 2022, a statue of Subhas Chandra

Bose was erected under the canopy on Kartavya Path (called Raj Path earlier). Netaji, 'the Leader', now stands taking the salute to not just the National War Memorial but to all future Republic Day parades. He had said 'Dilli Chalo' in 1943, and has finally arrived at the heart of the Republic.

Jai Hind! Vande Mataram!

About the Author

Sanjeev Sanyal is a writer, economist and urbanist. He grew up in Kolkata and attended Delhi University before going on to Oxford University as a Rhodes Scholar. He then spent two decades in international financial markets, where he became the managing director and global strategist of Europe's largest bank. He was named a Young Global Leader by the World Economic Forum in 2010. While living in Singapore, he also took up the study of cities and was awarded the Eisenhower Fellowship for his work on urban dynamics. In 2017, he joined the Indian government as the principal economic adviser. He became a member of Prime Minister Narendra Modi's economic advisory council in 2022. He has represented India in many international forums, including as co-chair of the Framework Working Group of G20 for five years.

His bestselling books for young readers include *The Incredible History of India's Geography*, *The Incredible History of the Indian Ocean* and *Iconic Indians*.

This book is an abridged edition of Sanjeev's *Revolutionaries: The Other Story of How India Won Its Freedom*, shortened and illustrated for young readers.